MURDER & MAYHEM ON CHICAGO'S SOUTH SIDE

MURDER & MAYHEM ON CHICAGO'S SOUTH SIDE

TROY TAYLOR

THE History PRESS

Published by The History Press
Charleston, SC 29403
www.historypress.net

Images are courtesy of the author unless otherwise noted.

First published 2009

Manufactured in the United States

ISBN 978.1.59629.697.8

Library of Congress Cataloging-in-Publication Data

Taylor, Troy.
Murder and mayhem on Chicago's South Side / Troy Taylor.
p. cm.
Includes bibliographical references.
ISBN 978-1-59629-697-8
1. Murder--Illinois--Chicago--History. 2. Crime--Illinois--Chicago--History. I. Title.
HV6534.C4T393 2009
364.152'3092277311--dc22
2009010457

Contents

Acknowledgements

I would like to thank my father for encouraging my interest in Chicago crime and giving me my first biography about Al Capone. Again, thanks to the many writers and chroniclers of crime in the Windy City, especially Herbert Asbury, Jay Robert Nash and Richard Lindberg, and to the kind keepers of libraries, history rooms and archives who always went out of their way to help. Thanks also to Jonathan Simcosky at The History Press and my wife, Haven, for always making sure that I know that nothing is too hard if I put my mind to it.

Introduction

Nobody planned Chicago. It was not laid out with care. It was carved from the mud, grass and muck along the shores of Lake Michigan and baptized with the blood of the first settlers and soldiers who came to what was then a desolate place. In 1803, those men established a fort called Fort Dearborn that was supposed to provide protection to the brave men and women who tried to build a home out of the wilderness. However, when the War of 1812 unleashed the fury of the Native Americans on the western frontier, Chicago almost ceased to exist before it got the chance to get started. In August 1812, the garrison at Fort Dearborn evacuated its post and, with women and children in tow, attempted to march to safety. But it was overwhelmed and wiped out, in a wave of bloodshed and fire, after traveling less than a mile to what is now the South Side of the city.

Fort Dearborn, which was originally built by Captain John Whistler, was constructed on a hill that loomed only about eight feet above the Chicago River. It was a simple stockade of logs, inside of which soldiers later built barracks, officers' quarters, a guardhouse and a small powder magazine of brick. West of the fort, they constructed a two-story log building to serve as an Indian agency, and between this structure and the fort they placed root cellars and gardens. Blockhouses were added at two corners of the fort and three pieces of light artillery were mounted there. The walls of the fort offered protection to the soldiers garrisoned there, and to the settlers who built homes nearby, but in the end they discovered that the feeling of protection was only an illusion.

An illustration of Fort Dearborn, circa 1803. *Courtesy of the Chicago Historical Society.*

At the start of the War of 1812, tensions in the wilderness began to rise. British troops came to the American frontier, spreading liquor and discontent among the Indian tribes, especially the Potawatomis, the Wyandots and the Winnebagos. In April 1812, an Indian raid occurred on the Lee farm, near Fort Dearborn, and two men were killed. After that, the fort became a refuge for many of the settlers and a growing cause of unrest for the local Indians. When war was declared that summer and the British captured the American garrison at Mackinac, it was decided that Fort Dearborn could not be held and the fort should be evacuated.

General William Hull, the American commander in the Northwest, issued orders to the fort's commander, Captain Nathan Heald, through Indian agent officers. Heald was told that the fort was to be abandoned; arms and ammunition were to be destroyed and all goods distributed to friendly Indians. Hull also sent a message to Fort Wayne, which sent Captain William Wells and a contingent of allied Miami Indians to Fort Dearborn to assist with the evacuation.

There is no dispute about whether General Hull gave the order, nor whether Captain Heald received it, but some have wondered if perhaps Hull's instruction, or his handwriting, was not clear because Heald waited eight days before acting on it. During that time, Heald argued with his officers, with local settlers who opposed the evacuation and with local Indians, one of whom fired a rifle in the commanding officer's quarters.

The delay gave the hostile Indians time to gather outside the fort. They assembled there in an almost siege-like state, and Heald realized that he was going to have to bargain with them if the occupants of Fort Dearborn were going to reach Fort Wayne safely. On August 13, all of the blankets, trading items and calico cloth were given out, and Heald held several councils with Indian leaders that his junior officers refused to attend.

Eventually, an agreement was reached that had the Indians providing safe conduct for the soldiers and settlers to Indiana. Part of the agreement was that Heald would leave the arms and ammunition in the fort for the Indians, but his officers refused to do this. Alarmed, they questioned the wisdom of handing out guns and ammunition that could easily be turned against them. Heald reluctantly went along with them, and the extra weapons and ammunition were broken apart and dumped into an abandoned well. Only twenty-five rounds of ammunition were saved for each man. As an added bit of insurance, all of the liquor barrels were smashed and the contents poured into the river during the night.

On August 14, Captain William Wells and his Miami allies arrived at the fort. Wells was a frontier legend among early soldiers and settlers in the Illinois territory. He was also the uncle of Captain Heald's wife, Rebekah, and after receiving the request for assistance from General Hull, he had headed straight to Fort Dearborn to aid in the evacuation. But even the arrival of the frontiersman and his loyal Miami warriors would not save the lives of those trapped inside Fort Dearborn.

Throughout the night of August 14, wagons were loaded for travel and the reserve ammunition was distributed. Early the next morning, the procession of soldiers, civilians, women and children left the fort. The infantry soldiers led the way, followed by a caravan of wagons and mounted men. A portion of the Miami men who had accompanied Wells guarded the rear of the column. It was reported that musicians played the dead march, a slow, solemn funeral march that forbode the disaster that followed.

The column of soldiers and settlers was escorted by nearly five hundred Potawatomi Indians. As they marched southward and into a low range of sand hills that separated the beaches of Lake Michigan from the prairie, the Potawatomis moved silently to the right, placing an elevation of sand between themselves and the white men from the fort. This act was carried out with such subtlety that no one noticed it as the column trudged along the shoreline.

The column traveled to what is now the near South Side, where Sixteenth Street and Indiana Avenue are located today. There was a sudden milling about of the scouts at the front of the line, and suddenly a shout came back from Captain Wells that the Indians were attacking. A line of Potawatomis appeared over the edge of the sand ridge and fired down at the column. Totally surprised, the officers nevertheless managed to rally the men into a battle line, but it was of little use. Soldiers fell immediately and the line collapsed. The Indians overwhelmed them with sheer numbers, flanking the line and snatching the wagons and horses.

What followed was butchery. Officers were slain with tomahawks, and the fort's surgeon was cut down by gunfire and then literally chopped into pieces. Rebekah Heald was wounded by gunfire but was spared when she was captured by a sympathetic Indian chief. The wife of one soldier fought so bravely and savagely that she was hacked into pieces before she fell. In the end, reduced to fewer than half their original number, the garrison surrendered under the promise of safe conduct. In all, 148 members of the column were killed; 86 adults and 12 children were slaughtered in the initial attack. The children had been loaded onto a single wagon for safety, and most were killed in one frenzied attack. The surrender that was arranged by Captain Heald did not apply to the wounded, and it is said that the Indians tortured them throughout the night and then left their bodies on the sand next to those who had already fallen.

Captain William Wells managed to kill eight Indians with his bare hands before he was felled and pinned down by his horse. Warriors pounced on him and killed him, then cut out his heart and ate it, hoping to ingest some of his ferocious bravery.

In the battle, Captain Heald was wounded twice, while his wife was wounded seven times. They were later released, and a St. Joseph Indian named Chaudonaire took them to Mackinac, where they were turned over to the British commander there. He sent them to Detroit, where they were exchanged with the American authorities.

After the carnage, the victorious Indians burned Fort Dearborn to the ground, and the bodies of the massacre victims were left where they had fallen, scattered to decay on the sand dunes of Lake Michigan. When replacement troops arrived at the site a year later, they were greeted with not only the burned-out shell of the fort but also the grinning skeletons of their predecessors. The bodies were given proper burial, and the fort was rebuilt and then abandoned a few years later when the city was able to fend for itself.

The story of the Fort Dearborn Massacre will be told for as long as Chicago stands and will always mark one of the bloodiest events in the history of the city.

After the war, more settlers came to the region, and in August 1833 Chicago was finally incorporated as a city. There is no record of how many people actually lived in Chicago at the time, but it is thought that the vote surrounding the incorporation might have been the first incident of voter fraud in the city's history, beginning a tradition that has stained Chicago's reputation ever since.

A preliminary vote was held on August 5, but only 13 actual voters turned out. Only one of them voted against incorporating, but since he lived up the South Branch, outside of the proposed city limits, his vote didn't count. The voters were invited to return to the polling place, known as Jolly Mark's Tavern, on August 10, and this time 28 people showed up. The rule of thumb in those days was that each voter represented 5 nonvoting people, meaning that Chicago had about 140 residents, at most. Unfortunately, a population of 150 residents was legally required before a city could become incorporated. In spite of this, the vote somehow went through and Chicago became an official city. It's no wonder that "vote early and vote often" became a slogan used to ridicule Chicago's voting habits in years to come.

In the years that followed, Chicago began to come into its own and was largely shaped by the influences that came from the city's South Side. The area became a commercial hub for manufacturing, meatpacking and transportation during the mid-nineteenth century. As more and more people came to the area, it also became a center for crime and the home to one of the most famous vice districts in the country.

In the early days, wealthy Chicagoans who wanted to live in secluded, spacious surroundings came to the South Side and built lavish dwellings near the Fort Dearborn Massacre site. The Prairie Avenue District, as it came to be called, was home to the cream of Chicago's society for decades. They were later pushed out by the rise of manufacturing—and crime—on the South Side and flocked to the Gold Coast in the early 1900s.

The Irish came to South Side Bridgeport in the 1840s and built the Illinois & Michigan Canal, the first waterway to link Chicago to the Illinois and Mississippi Rivers. The canal had been in the planning stages since the early days of Chicago, and thousands of mostly immigrant laborers managed to complete the nautical route by 1848. The canal opened up the city to the rest of the country and firmly established Chicago as an American commercial center.

The Prairie Avenue District was once home to Chicago's millionaires.

The streets of Bridgeport in the early 1900s. This largely Irish neighborhood on Chicago's South Side became home to the men who built the Illinois & Michigan Canal, as well as street gangs, local toughs and a number of Chicago's mayors.

In 1865, John Sherman opened stockyards on Chicago's South Side that went on to earn the city both acclaim and infamy. Carl Sandburg called Chicago the "hog butcher for the world," but it was actually beef that made the city wealthy. Until the 1800s, cuts of beef were prepared only by local butchers. However, in 1872, a man named Gustavas Swift began buying cattle from the western ranges and shipping sides of beef to the East on express trains that ran in the winter months with their doors open to preserve the butchered meat. Later, Swift developed refrigerated rail cars, and soon he and his chief competitor, Phillip Armour, were shipping most of the nation's beef and pork products.

Both men established companies in an area on the South Side that was often referred to as "Packingtown," named for the tenement housing near the stockyards. The workers lived in these run-down slums, receiving pay so poor that many of the children in the area scavenged for food from the garbage dumps. The slaughterhouses were filthy and dangerous places to work, and the workers were treated with little regard. The waste from the slaughtering was dumped into an open sewer that ran through Packingtown into what was called "Bubbly Creek." Filled with greasy sewage, the creek was supposed to have a scum so thick that men often joked that a steer could walk on it without sinking.

In the late 1800s, the horrific conditions of Packingtown caught the attention of Frank Warren, the editor of a weekly Socialist newspaper. He

A scene from the Chicago meatpacking district on the South Side.

decided to send one of his reporters, a young man named Upton Sinclair, into the district to write an exposé on the packinghouses. Sinclair was an impoverished writer, and his threadbare clothing helped him to blend in with the workers in Packingtown. He found that by carrying a pail with him, he could get into anywhere that he wanted to go. His investigation turned into a newspaper series that started in February 1905. He later expanded the pieces into a novel titled *The Jungle*, which was published by Doubleday in 1906. The graphic accounts shocked readers, and the book sold more than 100,000 copies the first year it was in publication.

One admirer of the book was President Theodore Roosevelt, who had long been a critic of the nation's meatpackers. During the Spanish-American War, he stated that he would rather eat his old hat than consume the meat that the packing companies sent to Cuba. Roosevelt began actively pursuing government regulations of the meatpacking industry, including thorough inspections of the factories where the meat was being slaughtered and processed. The meatpackers opposed the new standards, but with sales falling in the wake of Sinclair's book, they had no choice but to let inspectors into their plants. The unsanitary conditions the inspectors found turned the public against the industry. A popular rhyme that made the rounds in Chicago in 1906 went: "Mary had a little lamb, and when she saw it sicken, she shipped it off to Packingtown, and now it's labeled chicken."

President Roosevelt pushed ahead with his plans, and the first meat inspection bill was passed one year later. A novel had changed an entire industry, and meatpacking was never the same again.

In 1893, Chicago's South Side played host to the World's Columbian Exposition, celebrating the 400th anniversary of Christopher Columbus's landing in America. Chicago, New York, Washington and St. Louis all competed vigorously for the honor of hosting the fair, and it was during this jockeying that the city of Chicago actually gained the title of the "Windy City." As Chicago was doing more boasting about its landscape and amenities than any of the other cities, Charles A. Dana, editor of the *New York Sun*, advised his readers to ignore the "nonsensical claims of that windy city." This was the first use of the term, and it had nothing to do with wind gusts along Lake Michigan.

The fair was a great success for the city of Chicago and for the city's burgeoning crime and vice elements as well. Attendance at the gin joints and brothels of the South Side Levee tripled, and everyone seemed to be making money. The city also attracted many famous, and infamous, visitors,

The 1893 World's Columbian Exposition in Chicago attracted hundreds of thousands of people to the city's South Side, including criminals and purveyors of every kind of vice imaginable.

including Gentleman Jim Corbett, Diamond Jim Brady, John Philip Sousa, Lillian Russell and many others. The fairgrounds that were constructed on the shoreline of Lake Michigan comprised more than 630 acres and attracted an attendance that equaled nearly half of the population of America at that time. The grounds included palaces, lagoons and immense buildings of plaster. Many of them became electrically lighted fantasies at night and so gleamed in the daylight sun that the grounds were dubbed the "White City."

But not everything was pristine and beautiful with the Columbian Exposition. Despite the public face that had been put on the event, a darker side lurked just below the surface. The area was a prime target for confidence men, pea-shell and three-card Monte men and thieves of every kind. Newspapers reported muggings and robberies, country yokels who were conned by loaded dice, marked cards, the gin joints and the prostitutes, who could easily be found within walking distance of the fairgrounds.

The criminal underworld of the South Side was well defined by the mid-1800s. Irish and Italian thugs organized as gangs and tapped into ward politics as a source of strength. They spread terror through extortion, gambling rackets and sporting houses. The questionable alliance between criminals and politicians allowed vice to flourish in the notorious Levee District. The Levee attracted every sort of vice operation imaginable, including liquor, gambling and, notably, prostitution. It was known for its large number of brothels, including the famous house owned by the Everleigh sisters. The Levee defied the uptight conventions of the late Victorian era and went on to create opportunities for men like Al Capone who applied modern business principles to their criminal enterprises.

African Americans began arriving in Chicago in significant numbers before World War I, settling into the South Side area known as "Bronzeville," which ran west along Cottage Grove Avenue to Wentworth Avenue. After the war, the black community expanded, its population enlarged by trainloads of African Americans coming up from the Mississippi Delta on the Illinois Central line. Just as the white ethnic gangs had capitalized on the moral vagaries of the age, the black gangsters did the same, satisfying a growing demand for gambling and other kinds of vice. Bronzeville had the largest and most successful policy racket in America until the Chicago Outfit muscled in on the action in the late 1940s.

Years later, after the Capone mob and the policy kings had died, gone to prison or faded away, the South Side neighborhoods were taken over by drug traffickers and street gangs, turning the once stable and prosperous middle-class areas into blighted communities that remain stigmatized by their histories and reputations.

THE RISE AND FALL OF AL CAPONE

There is no name in Chicago history that is as recognizable as that of Al Capone. The South Side gang leader virtually ruled the city for years and amassed an unimaginable fortune during Prohibition. Capone's story actually begins with two of the most prominent criminals in pre-Prohibition Chicago, John Torrio and Jim Colosimo.

Torrio was born in Italy and came to New York as a child in 1884. His family settled on the Lower East Side, and while still in his early teens, Torrio led his own gang and gained a reputation for viciousness. More importantly, though, he gained a reputation for being intelligent and quick thinking. He never carried a gun—a fact that speaks volumes about him during a time when even the lowliest street thug carried at least one weapon—because he always surrounded himself with men who carried out his dirty work. By age twenty-two, he owned his own bar and whorehouse and became known as a fixer for politicians.

Torrio had a cousin in Chicago named Vittoria Moresco, who was one of the city's leading brothel keepers. In 1902, Vittoria married the flamboyant Jim Colosimo, an Italian who had worked his way up from cleaning streets to head the Street Laborer's Union and the City Streets Repairer's Union. At this point in his career, Colosimo was befriended by the two most powerful political bosses in Chicago: First Ward committeeman Michael Kenna and alderman John Coughlin. Within the First Ward lay the notorious Levee District, an area filled with whorehouses, saloons and gambling parlors. Kenna and Coughlin employed Colosimo as their collector in return for the votes of all of the

"Big Jim" Colosimo set the stage for organized crime in Chicago and brought John Torrio to the city. *Courtesy of the* Chicago Daily News.

members of his unions. This ensured his political clout and maintained his ability to operate his criminal enterprises without interference.

Colosimo's marriage to Torrio's cousin Vittoria made him even more prosperous. By 1912, he and his wife owned more than two hundred brothels, catering to all income levels. His base of operations, Colosimo's Café, was decorated in the most lavish style and was one of the most popular restaurants in Chicago. He entertained wealthy residents, city officials and even show business types like Enrico Caruso, the famous Italian tenor.

Colosimo's wealth made him a target for extortionists, and three different attempts were made on his life. In 1909, Vittoria convinced her husband to call John Torrio, her cousin in New York. Torrio took the train to Chicago and dealt with the extortionists by subcontracting two gunmen to kill them at the money drop. Torrio was asked to stay on in Chicago, and out of gratitude Colosimo put the young man in charge of his empire of saloons, whorehouses and gambling dens. In 1915, he also gave Torrio permission to set up his own criminal organization. Torrio purchased a building at 2222 South Wabash Avenue, which would be known from then on by the number of its address, the Four Deuces. Torrio set up a brothel on the top floor, gambling operations on the second and third and a bar at street level. The Four Deuces soon became the headquarters for a criminal enterprise far beyond anything that Colosimo could have imagined. Within a short time, Torrio was controlling over one thousand enterprises that were all devoted to drinking, gambling or sex. His stable of gunmen eliminated anyone who opposed him.

When Prohibition arrived in 1920, Torrio was determined to profit from the opportunities that it presented. He soon realized that the only way for his organization to operate was by sitting down with rival gangs and marking out territory; otherwise the battle to supply illegal liquor to the thousands of speakeasies that sprang up would lead to chaos and ongoing war. He went to his mentor, Colosimo, and presented his plans to him.

Colosimo, though, was not interested in Torrio's plans. At the time, he was distracted by his romantic interest in a woman named Dale Winters, a young musical comedy actress who had been stranded in Chicago after an unsuccessful theatrical tour. She accepted an invitation to perform in one of Colosimo's establishments, and the two fell in love. In 1920, he divorced his wife and married Dale three weeks later. Torrio was astonished to find that Colosimo couldn't be bothered to protect his operations from his rivals. This left only one solution to the problem in Torrio's mind: Colosimo had to be eliminated.

The notorious Four Deuces was the headquarters for the Torrio-Capone gang on the South Side. *Courtesy of the Chicago Historical Society.*

On the afternoon of May 11, 1920, Colosimo left for his restaurant with plans to meet his new wife later that night for dinner. When he arrived, he went to his office and spoke with his secretary, Frank Camilla, who had been meeting with the chef about that evening's dinner. Colosimo spoke with them for a few minutes and then, about 4:30 p.m., he allegedly took a telephone call from Johnny Torrio, who explained that a shipment of whiskey was being delivered to the restaurant and that Colosimo had to sign for it personally. Colosimo left the office and walked out into the lobby. A moment later, two shots were fired. Frank Camilla went to investigate the sounds and found Colosimo's dead body lying on the floor of the lobby with a bullet wound in the back of the head. The second bullet was lodged in the plaster wall. From the angle of the shots, the killer, the police concluded, must have been hiding in the cloakroom.

The funeral of Big Jim Colosimo was held on May 15 and was the first of the gaudy burial displays that were the fashion in Chicago's underworld throughout the 1920s. Thousands attended, including both gangsters and politicians, further underscoring the alliances between the two.

After Colosimo's death, Torrio immediately took over the dead man's entire operation. He had an army of between seven and eight hundred men working for him, but he always had room for more. One of the soldiers he recruited was a young man from Brooklyn whom he had known since he was fourteen. In 1921, Torrio invited this man to come to Chicago and work for him. His name was Alphonse Capone.

Capone was born in Naples, Italy, in 1899, and his parents immigrated to America shortly after the turn of the century. The family—father, mother, five sons and one daughter—settled in Brooklyn. As a child, Capone was given little education and almost no parental supervision. As he grew older, he made a name for himself as a slugger and a gunman with the famous Five Pointers gang in New York, of which several of his cousins were members. In his final days in Brooklyn, friends remembered him as a good-looking, affable, soft-spoken young man, distinguished only by his flashy clothes and skill as a dancer. His good looks were marred in a tangle with a knife-wielding Sicilian that left a long scar on his left cheek that ran from the top of his ear to the corner of his mouth.

Capone started out on the bottom rung of the ladder in Chicago, working as a promoter outside one of Torrio's whorehouses. At that time, Capone met Jake Guzik, a member of a large Jewish family involved in prostitution. They became friends, and Guzik went on to become the treasurer for the

Al Capone, "King of Chicago." *Courtesy of the Chicago Historical Society.*

Torrio-Capone organization. Capone's esteem for Guzik was clearly shown in 1924, when Joe Howard, a hijacker, made an anti-Semitic remark to Guzik. Capone shot Howard six times in front of witnesses in a saloon on South Wabash Avenue. Capone was interrogated about the shooting by Assistant State's Attorney William McSwiggin but was released for lack of evidence after all of the witnesses developed memory loss.

In 1922, Capone became Torrio's first lieutenant and the chief of his gunmen. They took over a number of breweries and then began to organize the major Chicago gangs, assigning each its own territory. In return, the gangs forced saloons to stock Torrio alcohol and also protected shipments and assisted distribution. The North Side of the city fell to Dion O'Banion. The West Side was divided between Terry Druggan and Frankie Lake, leaders of the Valley Gang. Torrio controlled the South Side, and the rest was divided among mobsters Ralph Sheldon, Danny Stanton, Frank McErlane and Joe Saltis.

Two gangs left out of Torrio's syndicate were the Klondike O'Donnell gang, based in Cicero, and the unrelated O'Donnell brothers, led by Spike O'Donnell, who at the time was in prison for bank robbery. When he got out, Spike began hijacking Torrio's trucks and moving in on the territory of Frank McErlane and Joe Saltis. Spike O'Donnell and his men were massacred and driven out of the city between 1923 and 1925.

In 1923, Torrio and Capone, motivated by the election of a reform mayor, William E. Dever, who closed down thousands of speakeasies, decided to move their headquarters from the Four Deuces to the Hawthorne Inn, located in the suburb of Cicero. This independent township was outside the jurisdiction of the mayor of Chicago. The area was dominated by the Western Electric plant, which paid its employees well, meaning that the local populace had plenty of money to spend in the gambling parlors and saloons. Cicero also had a large number of Czech immigrants, who were accustomed to thick, Bohemian beer. This was supplied by the West Side O'Donnells, who had not joined the Torrio-Capone syndicate.

Torrio struck a deal with them, and soon the South Side gang was firmly entrenched in Cicero. Soon after, Torrio left everything in Capone's hands and traveled to Italy with his mother and several million dollars. He bought his mother a villa and deposited the money in an Italian bank. He then returned to Chicago.

The first challenge that awaited Capone in Cicero was taking over the city government. His chance came with the mayoral election of 1924 between Democrat Rudolph Hurt and Republican Joseph Z. Klenha. The election took place on April 1, and Capone threw the weight of the syndicate behind Klenha. By this time, Capone had brought his entire family to Chicago, and his brothers, Ralph and Frank, helped bring out the vote for Klenha and other syndicate candidates. They were assisted in this task by more than two hundred gunmen, who stationed themselves at polling booths and made sure

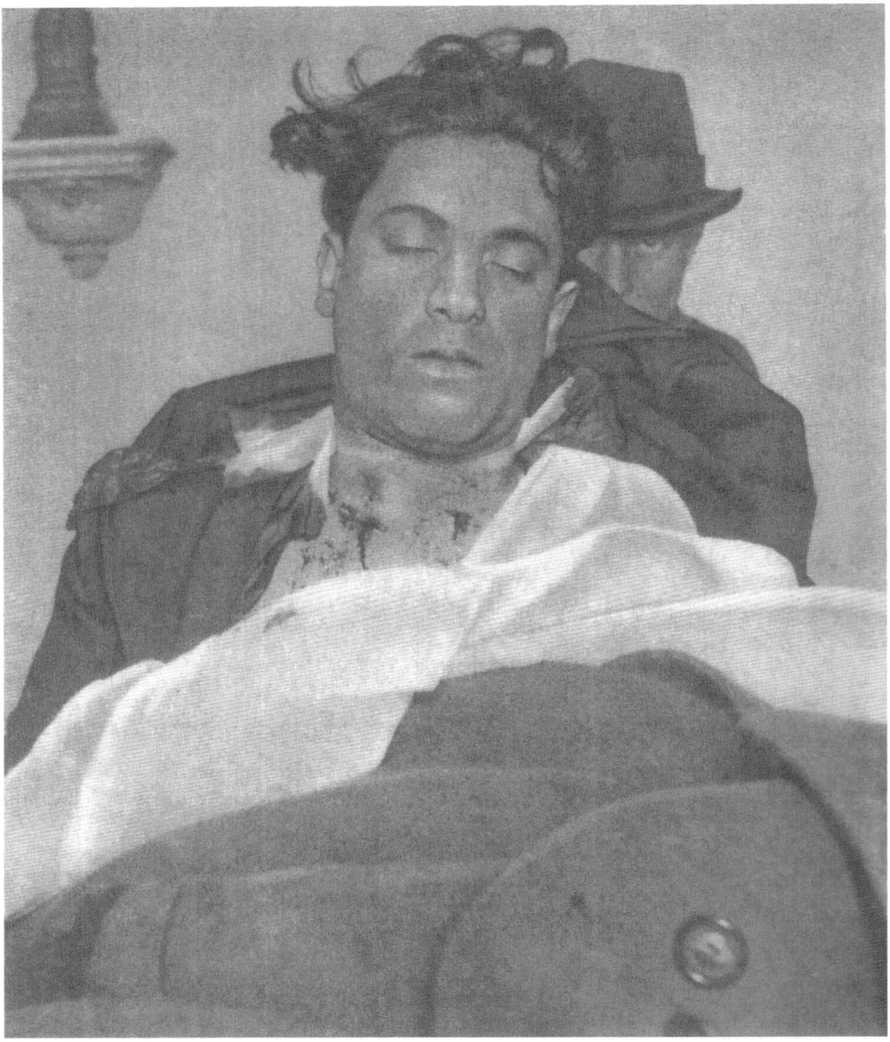

Frank Capone was killed during election day violence in Cicero in 1924. *Courtesy of the* Chicago Daily News.

that voters only cast ballots for the candidates of choice. Those who opposed them were violently beaten, and those who went along were allowed to vote as many times as they wished.

News of the violence and voter fraud reached county judge Edmund K. Jarecki, who ordered seventy policemen to go into Cicero and stop it.

They wore plainclothes and arrive in unmarked cars. As they drove past the Western Electric plant, the first mobster they spotted was Frank Capone. The officers stopped and jumped out of their cars. Frank, thinking that they had come to kill him, reached for his gun and was cut down by shotgun blasts before he could get to it. The police then emptied their revolvers into his body as he lay bleeding on the street.

Frank was twenty-nine years old and was given a magnificent gangland funeral. He was placed in a silver-plated casket, and the modest Capone home on South Prairie Avenue was filled with more than $20,000 worth of flowers. A procession of one hundred cars took the casket to Mount Carmel Cemetery. Capone had lost a brother, but he had won the election. The mob was now in charge of Cicero.

Not long after Capone made inroads into Cicero politics, trouble began to brew in Chicago. Problems had started to develop between Torrio-Capone ally Dion O'Banion, leader of an eccentric legion of mostly Irish gunmen, and the Gennas, a family of Sicilian brothers from Taylor Street who supplied

Capone's modest two-flat home on South Prairie Avenue. The house still stands today as one of the last remaining relics of the Capone era in Chicago. *Courtesy of the Chicago Historical Society.*

Torrio with poorly made liquor that was manufactured in neighborhood stills. The Gennas had started selling their cheap whiskey on the North Side of Chicago, O'Banion's territory, in a clear infringement of the agreement that had been made. O'Banion complained to Torrio, who was reluctant

Dion O'Banion, the eccentric leader of Chicago's North Side gang. Along with Hymie Weiss and George "Bugs" Moran, he used political influence and violence to control operations in his part of the city.

to intervene. The Gennas were extremely violent and politically well connected, so Torrio did not want to provoke them. Impatient, O'Banion hijacked a Genna delivery truck in retaliation. Torrio used his diplomatic skills to keep the Gennas from violence but couldn't stop them from flooding other territories with their liquor. O'Banion was fed up, and it was clear that the Torrio truce was breaking down.

O'Banion went on the offensive, selling his beer and liquor all over the South Side. Torrio constantly tried to negotiate with him rather than use the violence that Capone began to urge. Dozens of meetings were held between Torrio, Capone and O'Banion, and each ended with the same results. O'Banion always promised to recognize the territory of the South Side operation, but he never kept the promise. The Gennas wanted to hit O'Banion and so did Capone, but Torrio asked them to wait. Torrio knew that if he killed O'Banion, it would mean all-out war in Chicago.

Unfortunately for Torrio, his hesitation to move against O'Banion led to his arrest on liquor charges. O'Banion convinced Torrio that he wanted to sell off one of his whiskey distilleries, and when Torrio arrived to inspect the property, Police Chief Collins, leading twenty officers, raided the place and arrested O'Banion, Earl "Hymie" Weiss and Torrio. O'Banion and Weiss escaped serious charges, but this was Torrio's second arrest for violating Prohibition, which meant that he would be serving mandatory jail time. It was time, Torrio finally decided, to get rid of O'Banion.

On November 10, 1924, O'Banion was shot to death in a flower shop that he owned in downtown Chicago. The Genna brothers, Capone and Torrio were all questioned about the murder, but all were released after supplying airtight alibis. The investigation, headed by ace detective Captain William "Shoes" Shoemaker, went nowhere.

O'Banion's death ignited an all-out war in Chicago. A few days after the gang leader's lavish funeral, the first of a dozen or more attempts were made to kill Capone. Gunmen in a closed car overtook his limousine one evening, crowded it to the curb and raked it with bullets from front to back. Luckily, Capone was not in the automobile at the time. His driver was seriously injured.

Two months later, Torrio was shot twice outside of his home at 7011 Clyde Avenue. He survived the attack and, in February, was prosecuted on Prohibition charges and sentenced to serve nine months at the Waukegan County Jail. When Torrio got out of prison, he decided to turn his operations over to Capone and leave Chicago for good. He spent time in Italy and then moved to New York, where he went into the real estate business with the blessing of Meyer Lansky and Charles "Lucky" Luciano. He also helped to establish a liquor cartel along the Atlantic seaboard and established himself as an elder statesman of the underworld. He died (of natural causes) in a barber's chair in 1957.

Torrio's departure from Chicago shoved Al Capone into the violent spotlight of the Chicago underworld, and it made him the top man in the city at only twenty-five years of age. He had a lavish lifestyle, more money than he could spend and a bloody gang war on his hands. The new leader of the O'Banion operation, Hymie Weiss, offered to stem further violence by having Capone hand over John Scalise and Albert Anselmi to him. It was a poorly kept secret that the two Capone mobsters had been in the flower shop when O'Banion was murdered. Capone refused and tried to knock off Hymie Weiss instead. He was ambushed on Michigan Avenue in the middle of the afternoon but, despite a storm of machine-gun fire, escaped unharmed.

Weiss and former O'Banion sidekick George "Bugs" Moran retaliated next. On May 26, 1925, they murdered Angelo Genna, one of Capone's supporters. A month later, Mike Genna was killed by the police as he, John Scalise and Albert Anselmi were about to ambush George Moran. Scalise and Anselmi killed two police officers before escaping. Tony Genna was murdered soon after by the Gennas' own gunman, Giuseppe Nerone, who Moran may have paid to assassinate him. The surviving Gennas soon left for Italy.

Hymie Weiss struck again on September 20, 1926. Capone was sitting in the restaurant of the Hawthorne Hotel in Cicero when the next assassination attempt took place. With the street outside packed with shoppers and automobiles, no one noticed as cars filled with North Side gangsters slowly cruised down Twenty-Second Street. One of the cars accelerated away from the others, and as it passed the restaurant, black barrels of machine guns appeared from the windows and opened fire. Glass shattered and wood splintered as bullets riddled the restaurant. The car sped off, but it was followed by eight more touring cars, also filled with men and machine guns. They opened fire, emptying their guns into the hotel, spraying everything in sight. Over one thousand rounds were fired into the building and every window in the place was shattered. Amazingly, no one was killed. Capone escaped injury by lying facedown on the floor of the restaurant until the barrage was over.

Two months later, Capone's driver was taken on a "one-way ride." His mutilated body, found in an abandoned cistern, provided evidence of the fact that he had been tortured by someone who was looking for information about Capone's whereabouts and habits.

Hymie Weiss took over O'Banion's operations after his boss was killed in November 1924. He made several attempts on the life of Al Capone but was finally killed in October 1926 in front of Holy Name Cathedral. *Courtesy of the* Chicago Daily News.

Soon after the driver's body was discovered, Capone made another attempt to get Hymie Weiss, and this time he succeeded. On October 11, Weiss was attending the murder trial of "Polack Joe" Saltis and his driver, Frank "Lefty" Koncil, and decided to take a break and return to his office above O'Banion's old flower shop. As Weiss and gunman Patrick Murray drove toward the office, they had no idea that four machine gunners were waiting for them. The gunmen were hiding on the third floor of a nearby building, and when Weiss left his car on Superior Street, just south of Holy Name Cathedral, they opened fire. Patrick Murray died instantly, but Weiss took ten bullets and survived long enough to be pronounced dead at Henrotin Hospital without regaining consciousness. No one was ever prosecuted for these daylight murders.

The underworld battles continued. Gangsters were killed in their homes, on city streets, in doorways and behind the wheels of their automobiles. The Chicago press reported that between 1923 and 1926 there were 135 mob killings in the city. Most of the murders were unsolved, although there were investigations, a dozen or more arrests and a half dozen indictments and trials.

During all of this bloodshed, Capone's business expanded and prospered. He acquired interests in a number of dog-racing tracks in Cook County and broke into the labor union racket. He also claimed a share of the protection racket and imposed on owners of laundries, restaurants and other small businesses compulsory insurance against bombings. And, of course, his alcohol, gambling and prostitution operations continued to bring in tremendous amounts of money.

In December 1926, Capone went to New York to negotiate with Frankie Yale over the purchase of Canadian whiskey. After business was completed, Yale invited Capone to stay for a Christmas Eve party at the Adonis Social & Athletic Club in Brooklyn. Yale warned Capone that there might be trouble, as the White Handers, an Irish gang led by Richard "Peg Leg" Lonegran, had threatened to attack the party, but Capone agreed to stay in New York. The issue between Yale and the Irish was control of the Brooklyn docks, a traditionally Irish stronghold that was now threatened by Yale's gang.

Lonegran and his men arrived at the club on Christmas Eve, demanding drinks and making insulting remarks to the Italians who had gathered for the party. As they stood at the bar, the owner of the place suddenly turned off all the lights and then buried a meat cleaver in the skull of one of the Irishmen. Shots rang out, and when the lights were turned back on, three more of Lonegran's men were dead. Lonegran, who had lost his wooden leg, was hiding under a piano. He emptied his gun at Capone, who walked over and shot him three times in the head. Capone was charged with murder, but the indictment was dismissed and Capone was back in Chicago by the New Year. What was later referred to as the "Adonis Club Massacre" changed the balance of power not only on the Brooklyn docks, which fell under control of the Italians, but also between Brooklyn and Chicago. Both Torrio and Capone had come out of Brooklyn, and in some respects their operation was a Brooklyn subsidiary. By killing Lonegran, Capone had established the dominance of his Chicago organization over Brooklyn.

Soon after Capone returned to Chicago, he moved his operation into another area, the largely Italian suburb of Chicago Heights. At the time, it was controlled by a group of Sicilians who ran a protection racket on home distillers. Capone's men killed off the Sicilians and he took over their operation.

Capone was now running Chicago Heights, but this was not the best news that he would receive in the spring of 1927. In April, reform mayor William E. Dever lost the election to gangland's favorite candidate, William Hale Thompson. Capone had sponsored "Big Bill" with over $250,000 of his own money because he knew that with Thompson in office, he could literally rule the city. According to legend, Capone had three framed portraits over the desk in his office: George Washington, Abraham Lincoln and "Big Bill" Thompson.

A month later, in May 1927, as a result of the court case *United States v. Sullivan*, the United States Supreme Court passed an unusual law. The law stated that profits from the illegal sale of alcohol could be taxed like any other income. Although the law seemed ridiculous, it became a powerful law enforcement tool against bootleggers. No one was going to readily admit that he was engaged in illegal activity and making money from it, but if the police could prove that someone was a bootlegger by raiding his operation, the bootlegger could be sent to jail for not filing income tax returns. And if he filed an income tax return, he implicated himself in an illegal act. The U.S. attorney's office in Chicago estimated that Al Capone had grossed over $105 million from bootlegging, vice and gambling, but he had never filed a single tax return.

Soon after Mayor Thompson took office, four unsolved murders took place, all linked to Capone. Each of the dead men had been shot to death and was found with a nickel clenched in his hand. Rumor had it that the

William "Big Bill" Thompson set the standard for crooked politicians in Chicago. He was revered by Al Capone.

dead men were out-of-town mobsters who had come to Chicago to kill Al Capone. Before they could, each was taken out by Capone's favorite gunman, "Machine Gun" Jack McGurn. The nickel was McGurn's calling card. When he was a boy, his father had been killed by the Gennas and they had laughed about his death, calling McGurn's father a "nickel and dime man." McGurn had sworn revenge against them. When he grew up and started working as a gunman for Capone, he had the chance to kill the Gennas, and each time he did, he left a nickel in the corpse's hand.

The 1927 murder victims were believed to be gangsters hoping to collect a $50,000 bounty that was placed on Capone's head by Joseph Aiello, a Sicilian and rival gangster. Aiello and his brothers, Antonio, Dominick and Andrew, ran a numbers racket and levied a tax on California grapes unloaded in Chicago railroad sidings. After failing to kill Capone using hired gunmen, Aiello next tried to bribe one of his cooks to poison him. This also failed when the chef informed Capone of the attempt. When Capone discovered that Aiello had then set up a machine-gun position across the street from the store where Capone made payoffs, Capone informed friends on the police force, who arrested Aiello and suggested that he leave town. Capone later had Aiello gunned down in New Jersey.

In early 1928, Capone and his family left Chicago for Miami. Toward the end of 1927, Capone had repeatedly stated in public that he planned to retire from bootlegging, even calling a press conference to announce his intentions to a skeptical group of reporters. In Florida, he purchased a house in the name of his wife, Mae, on Palm Island, near Miami. The purchase attracted the attention of the Internal Revenue Service, which was determined to go after Capone for nonpayment of income tax. Relentless IRS agents investigated the sale, but because the house was in Mae's name, they were unable to use it to indict Capone. They were stunned to discover that even though Capone had a lavish lifestyle, they could not connect an income greater than the allowable exemption of $5,000 to the mobster.

On July 1, 1928, Capone was responsible for one of the most significant gangland assassinations of the year: the murder of New York gangster Frankie Yale. Yale had started out as a member of a gang in the Five Points neighborhood with Johnny Torrio in 1908. In 1918, after having proven his mob credentials, he took over the Unione Siciliana, which had evolved from a fraternal order into a criminal organization. Based out of the Harvard Inn at Coney Island, Yale started in the bootlegging business when Prohibition went into effect in 1920. Yale supplied Capone's liquor needs in Chicago and was

In 1928, Capone arranged the assassination of Frankie Yale in New York. The two men had been friends but had had a falling out over business. *Courtesy of the* Chicago Daily News.

also on call to perform assassinations for him if needed. The two men had a falling out after Yale tried to take over the Chicago branch of the Unione Siciliana. In addition, Capone believed that Yale was hijacking his own whiskey shipments to Capone and blaming the revenue loss on rival gangsters.

Capone sent four gunmen to Brooklyn, and on July 1, 1928, they followed Yale's bulletproof car and shot-gunned him through the window. They finished the job with a Thompson submachine gun, marking the first time that a "tommy gun" was used in New York. Yale's speeding car crashed into the front of a house, and his bloody and bullet-ridden body was thrown out onto the sidewalk. Yale's killers threw their guns away after the murder, as was the custom, but they were later recovered by the police. Investigators traced the guns back to Capone, who denied any knowledge of the crime. Since this was the only evidence that they had against the killers, no indictments against Capone, or his gunmen, were ever returned.

A few weeks after Yale's murder, Capone left his wife and son in Florida and returned to Chicago. He set up new headquarters on the South Side at the Lexington Hotel, first renting ten rooms and eventually taking over most of the hotel.

Around this time, he saw the first repercussions for the killing of Frankie Yale. Capone's candidate for the presidency of the Unione Siciliana, Antonio "Tony" Lombardo, was killed. His murder was committed during the evening rush hour on the "world's busiest corner," the corner of State

Antonio "Tony" Lombardo was murdered during rush hour on one of downtown Chicago's busiest corners. His killers were never caught. *Courtesy of the* Chicago Daily News.

and Madison in downtown Chicago. Lombardo and two of his bodyguards were walking along a crowded sidewalk when two men pressed up against them. The crack of revolver shots was heard and Lombardo and his men fell to the ground, victims of one of the boldest gang killings in Chicago history. Lombardo died instantly, with two bullets in his brain. One of the guards, mortally wounded, died soon afterward. The other guard was wounded but survived, although he was unable to give a description of the assailants. As usual, there were no arrests.

The successor to the presidency of the Unione Siciliana, Pasqualino Lolardo, was murdered in his home on January 8, 1929. Two men called on him and sat down at a table with food and wine. A toast was offered in honor of Lolardo and then two shots were fired, killing him on the spot. *Courtesy of the* Chicago Daily News.

Lombardo's successor, Pasqualino Lolardo, also a friend of Capone's, was killed in January 1929. His murder was also thought to be in retaliation for the death of Frankie Yale.

The killings for the domination of the Unione Siciliana made up a small part of the gang slaughter that occurred in the late 1920s. There was an unbroken succession of killings, sometimes numbering as many as fourteen mysterious murders every month. Some were Capone men and some were remnants of the old O'Banion gang, now called the "Bugs" Moran gang. Others were rival beer makers and sellers, rival whiskey runners, rival hijackers and rivals in the labor racket.

Capone, although known to be in Florida, was justly (and sometimes unjustly) credited with having a hand in all of the murders. The most famous of all of these killings occurred in February 1929 and was undoubtedly the work of Al Capone. His problems with the North Side gangsters had never gone away and Capone was determined to rid himself of George "Bugs" Moran. On February 14, 1929, he arranged a massacre to take place at the S-M-C Cartage Company, a garage on North Clark Street. Seven men were killed that morning, but Capone missed Moran. Regardless, the St. Valentine's Day Massacre, as it came to be called, marked the end of any significant gang opposition to Capone. Unfortunately for the South Side outfit, it also became the event that finally marked the beginning of the end of Capone's criminal empire. The massacre started a wave of reform that would eventually send him out of power for good.

Capone was conveniently still in Florida when the St. Valentine's Day Massacre took place. He was photographed on February 14 with all-American football player Bill Cunningham and pugilist Jack Sharkey at a Miami resort. *Courtesy of the* Chicago Daily News.

Capone returned to Chicago in May 1929. On May 8, the bodies of John Scalise, Albert Anselmi and Unione Siciliana President Joseph "Hop Toad" Guinta were found near a gangland dumping ground called Wolf Lake, located southeast of the city. They had apparently been taken on one of the mob's infamous "one-way rides." The beaten and bullet-riddled bodies of the three men were discovered inside a car that had been dumped into a ditch on an undeveloped part of Wolf Lake property, just across the Indiana border. The murders were never solved, but all three had been questioned in connection to the St. Valentine's Day Massacre. Some believe that remnants of the North Side mob may have killed them.

Others theorize that the men were murdered by Al Capone himself. Informants allegedly told him that Scalise, Anselmi and Guinta had allied themselves with Capone's old enemy, Joseph Aiello. Capone, after corroborating the rumor, invited the three men, along with about one hundred other guests, to a gangland banquet. After dinner was over, Capone savagely beat the three men to death with a baseball bat and then his gunmen shot them to pieces. The story has never been verified.

John Scalise (middle) and Albert Anselmi (second from right) were questioned by detectives after the murder of Tony Genna in 1925. The two men, both Capone gunmen, were found murdered in May 1929. *Courtesy of the* Chicago Daily News.

A few days later, on May 10, Capone went to New Jersey, accompanied by Anthony "Joe Batters" Accardo. In Atlantic City, they met with crime leaders from all over the country who were concerned about the bad publicity that Capone had generated. The guests included Meyer Lansky, Charles "Lucky" Luciano, Albert Anastasia, Frank Costello and Capone's old mentor, John Torrio. The New York contingent was upset with Capone not only for the massacre on St. Valentine's Day, but also for killing Frankie Yale without permission—and for having the gall to do it in New York territory.

The delegates talked for three days, often walking on the beach, where they could be far away from prying ears. They adopted a series of resolutions, some designed to cut Capone down to size and others to lay groundwork for organized crime after Prohibition. The delegates also formed a commission, with retired Torrio as the head, that would deal with all disagreements between members. Capone's organization was to be disbanded immediately and his gambling joints taken over by the commission. There would be no more killing, and the new head of the Chicago Unione Siciliana would be Capone's enemy, Joseph Aiello.

It was also agreed that it would be good public relations if Al Capone went to jail for a time. It was arranged for him to be arrested in Philadelphia on a charge of carrying a concealed weapon. Two detectives were paid to arrest him in the lobby of a movie theatre, charge him and get him sentenced as quickly as possible. It all happened in just sixteen hours, and he was sentenced to spend a term of one year at the Eastern State Penitentiary.

Capone's confinement was without the usual prison restrictions. He was allowed to make regular long-distance telephone calls to Jake Guzik in Chicago and to use the warden's office for private conferences with his Philadelphia attorneys. The lawyers were often joined by Guzik, Frank Nitti and Ralph Capone.

Capone was released on March 17, 1930. He had served his full sentence with the prescribed time off for good behavior. When Capone returned to Chicago, he was still at the height of his wealth and power, but he found that the climate of the city had changed. His popularity had waned, and the police were adamant about putting his operations out of business. Police Captain John Stege even posted a guard of twenty-five policemen in front of the Capone home on South Prairie Avenue with orders to arrest him as soon as he arrived from Pennsylvania. Capone slipped quietly into the city, though, and took up residence at the Hawthorne Inn in Cicero, where he spent four days answering mail and getting caught up on the state of operations. Then, he and his attorneys blatantly called on Captain Stege and the United States district attorney and found that neither of them had an actual warrant for his arrest. With that settled, he moved into the Lexington Hotel on the South Side.

Capone was greeted with more bad news when he got out of prison. His brother, Ralph, who had been left in charge of operations, had been indicted for income tax evasion. However, Capone discounted the problems that his brother was having. It seemed unlikely that anyone would be convicted of a crime as small as not paying taxes. But the government's strategy was a sound one. Juries that would never convict a gangster of murder, fearing retaliation, were much more likely to send him to prison over what was seen as little more than a bookkeeping error. Capone was stunned when Ralph was convicted and faced twenty-two years in prison.

Capone also found that a young Prohibition agent named Eliot Ness was making a nuisance of himself. Ness was born in Chicago in 1903 and was raised in the city. He graduated from the University of Chicago and, in 1928, joined the Bureau of Prohibition, working under the district attorney, George E.Q. Johnson. Ness began working undercover, posing as a corrupt official, in an investigation that resulted in eighty-six indictments and the destruction of a multimillion-dollar bootlegging operation.

Ness was then promoted and began trying to dismantle the Capone operation in Cicero. He soon found that the Prohibition Bureau was so riddled with corruption that little progress had been made against the bootleggers. Ness was determined to change that. He selected a small team of honest agents whose resistance to the Capone organization's efforts to buy them off led to their being dubbed the "Untouchables" by the newspapers. The chaos that Ness managed to create was carried out by just nine agents.

Ness tapped Ralph's telephone and learned the locations of some of the secret breweries that supplied the Capone organization. He raided a large brewery on South Wabash Avenue, ramming through the front door with a snowplow, and shut the place down, seizing hundreds of cases of beer. The team also managed to trace beer barrels on their journey from a speakeasy back to the brewery and was able to locate and raid six Capone breweries and five distribution plants. They seized twenty-five delivery trucks and confiscated beer worth about $9 million. To humiliate Capone, Ness drove the trucks past Capone's headquarters at the Lexington Hotel after calling the mob boss and telling him to look out the window.

"Untouchable" Eliot Ness, one of the men who helped to bring down Al Capone. *Courtesy of the Library of Congress.*

Ness managed to arrest sixty-nine Capone bootleggers, and his raids caused substantial damage to the organization. He survived several attempts on his life, once discovering a bomb in his car. In the end, it was not Ness's efforts alone that caused Capone's downfall, but they certainly contributed to it.

Capone may have been having trouble with the federal government, but he was still in charge of all operations in Chicago. The Atlantic City commission never enforced its sanctions against him, and when Capone returned from prison, he was able to take back control of the organization and continue things just as they had been before. Capone even went to the trouble of rubbing the syndicate's nose in the fact that it could do nothing to stop him by killing its appointed head of the Unione Siciliana, Joe Aiello. Aiello was shot and killed on Capone's orders, and the syndicate took no action against him.

During this time, a citizens' group called the Chicago Crime Commission published a list of the most prominent criminals in the city. The first name on the list was, of course, Al Capone. Capone was bothered by the list, since it seemed to show how far his popularity had slipped in the eyes of the general public. He began making efforts to try and undo some of the damage that had been done by the St. Valentine's Day Massacre. The U.S. stock market crashed on October 29, 1929, and by 1931, as the Great Depression worsened, hordes of the unemployed had appeared on the streets of Chicago. Capone tried to shrug off his "public enemy" image by opening a soup kitchen on South State Street during the winter months. On Thanksgiving Day alone he fed more than five thousand people. The goodwill that this generated did a great deal to soften Capone in the eyes of the ordinary Chicagoan, but it did nothing to help his image with the federal government. The government wanted to know where he got the money to pay for all of that generosity.

For years, investigators toiled endlessly to find proof of murder, bootlegging and racketeering committed by Al Capone. Nothing that they uncovered would stand up in court, so authorities instead began concentrating on his expenditures compared to his declared income. Internal Revenue Service agents blanketed stores in Chicago and Miami, calculating the cost of Capone's furniture, automobiles, tableware and clothing, right down to his underwear. After interviewing hundreds of people and looking over thousands of receipts, it was clear that Capone's income was vastly different than what he stated. Government agents were able to prove that Capone owed $215,080.48 in taxes. Capone offered to pay off the tax, but his offer was rejected. On June 5, 1931, he was indicted for income tax evasion. He was brought to trial on October 7 and convicted on five counts, three of evading taxes from 1925 to 1928 and two of failing to file tax returns in 1928 and 1929. He was sentenced to eleven years in prison and fined $80,000.

Capone was incarcerated at the Cook County Jail while he appealed his sentence. This allowed a number of public officials to repay past kindnesses that had been shown to them by Capone. Warden David Moneypenny installed him in a one-man cell on the fifth floor with a private shower. He was allowed to make telephone calls, send telegrams and continue running his operation from behind bars. However, anonymous telegrams that were sent to the Department of Justice, describing Capone's privileged life in jail, put an end to this treatment. After an investigation, Moneypenny was ordered to ban all visitors except the prisoner's wife, mother, son and lawyers. Capone was transferred to the hospital ward, with a detail of deputy U.S. marshals assigned to guard duty. On February 27, Capone learned that the district court had rejected his appeal.

Capone on his way into the courtroom in 1931. He was convicted of tax evasion and sent first to the federal penitentiary in Atlanta and later to Alcatraz. *Courtesy of Library of Congress.*

Capone's next appeal attempt was made to the U.S. Supreme Court, which rejected his application on May 2. On May 4, he was taken from the Cook County Jail. His original destination was Leavenworth, but since so many of Capone's men were already incarcerated there, officials decided that he should go to the Atlanta Penitentiary instead.

When Capone arrived at Atlanta, he was stripped to the skin and his clothing was replaced with a blue denim uniform. After being fingerprinted and photographed, his hair was shaved close to the skull, and he was transferred to the hospital ward for a three-week stay to determine if he carried any communicable diseases. Tests determined that Capone had syphilis, although Capone believed that he had been cured of it three years before. More tests were ordered, which included a spinal tap, but Capone refused them. It would later turn out that Capone did have the disease and, in fact, it was eating away at his brain. Toward the end of his life, it would utterly destroy him.

The overcrowded Atlanta Penitentiary had no single cells, only two-man and eight-man cells. Capone was assigned to an eight-man cell, whose occupants included an oil-well promoter, a former judge who had been convicted of mail fraud, a criminal from Ohio and four mail robbers serving twenty-five-year sentences. One of the mail robbers turned out to be Red Rudensky, a mechanic Capone knew from his early bootlegging days.

The other prisoners mostly admired Capone, and when Rudensky, who stage-managed most of the entertainment at the prison theatre, introduced him, Capone received a standing ovation. Rudensky remained close with Capone. He arranged the smuggling of cash to him from the gang by way of a trusty who drove a supply truck. With this money, Capone bought privileges from certain guards and loyalty and protection from other prisoners. He usually had a band of bodyguards who surrounded him at work and during recreation times in the yard.

Over the course of the next several months, Capone's family continued his legal battles on the outside, attempting to appeal his case. His attorney, William E. Leahy, was one of the most prominent lawyers in the country, and he attempted to reopen Capone's case, stating that the statute of limitations had run out. Capone appeared before federal judge E. Marvin Underwood, who took the petition under advisement. Capone was still waiting for the judge's decision when an announcement came that President Franklin D. Roosevelt had ratified the repeal of the Eighteenth Amendment. Prohibition had come to an end. This was, perhaps, a bad omen for Capone. Prohibition had allowed him to make all of the money for which he had gone to prison, and now it was over, just like Capone's final court case. The judge dismissed the petition and Capone remained in jail. And to make matters worse, word had just come from the Justice Department that he was going to be transferred to the brutal new "escape-proof" prison, Alcatraz.

Capone arrived at Alcatraz in August 1934. Upon his arrival, he quickly learned that while he may have once been famous, here he was only a number. He was arrogant after his stay in Atlanta, but he was soon to learn that things were much different at Alcatraz.

After Capone and the prisoners who arrived with him were unloaded from the train, they were taken to a low barge that brought them across the water to Alcatraz. When they arrived, they were led up a steep, twisting roadway to the top of the island. Warden James A. Johnston had a custom of meeting new prisoners when they arrived to give them a brief orientation. When Capone entered the rear of the cell house, Johnston sat at a desk. When he called out the names of the prisoners, a guard removed their handcuffs and brought them to the desk. Johnston later wrote in his memoirs that he had little trouble recognizing Capone when he saw him. Capone was grinning and making comments to other prisoners as he stood in the lineup. When it became his turn to approach the warden, Johnston ignored him and simply gave him a standard prison number, just like all of the other men. Johnston wrote:

> *It was apparent that he wanted to impress other prisoners by asking me questions as if he were their leader. I wanted to make sure that he didn't get any such idea. I handed him a ticket with his number, gave him the instructions I had given every other man, and told him to move along.*

The guards led Capone to the bathhouse to be stripped and medically examined and to have his ears, nose, mouth and rectum probed for contraband. For weekday wear, he was issued pants and a shirt made of gray denim and for Sunday, a blue denim uniform. For cold weather, he was given a wool-lined pea coat. The fronts and backs of his clothing were stamped with his number, "85," which could be seen from twenty yards away. After that, he was taken to his cell. The entire process, from the clothing to the accommodations, must have been quite a shock to the crime boss. Even in Atlanta, he had been used to special treatment, his own clothing, special food and drink and even silk underwear. He quickly discovered that Alcatraz was not the same sort of prison.

Warden Johnston had a policy to listen to any prisoner who wanted to speak with him, and he granted two separate interviews to Capone, who tried to inform the warden that he would be receiving a lot of visitors. Johnston explained to him that, like all of the other inmates, Capone had very limited visiting privileges, extending to blood relatives only, except for his brother, Ralph, who had a prison record. None of his "friends and business associates" was allowed to visit. No rules were going to be bent for any of the inmates, no matter who they were.

Johnston granted another interview request from Capone the following week, during which Capone again tried to plead his case for special visitors. He explained that among his important friends were big businessmen who depended on him for help and advice. Johnston again sent him on his way.

Capone may have struck out with the warden, but he was determined to try and gain the kind of leadership within the prison that he had enjoyed at Atlanta. Capone tried to dispense favors to his fellow prisoners, offering to have money sent to their relatives and to buy musical instruments for those who, like himself, wanted to play in the prison band. Johnston thwarted all of his efforts. When it became apparent that Capone could not obtain even the smallest consideration, he lost respect, as Johnston intended, among the inmates. He soon found that his safety was in danger.

It was deprivation of news from the outside world that led to Capone's first encounter with a punishment cell in the prison called the "hole." He spent a full nineteen days in the hole for attempting to bribe a guard to bring him a newspaper. He also did two ten-day stretches in the hole for talking to other inmates when the rule of silence was in effect. Each time that Capone was sent to the hole, he emerged a little worse for wear.

Capone was assigned to work in the prison's basement laundry room. The laundry room was damp and badly ventilated and the workload was often backbreaking. In January 1935, Capone was at his usual station when thirty-six of his co-workers walked off the job in protest. The strikers were quickly surrounded, separated and sent to the hole. Because Capone took no part in it, he aroused a great deal of hostility from the other workers. A month later, one of the strikers, Bill Collier, was catching laundry as Capone fed it into the machine. He complained that it was coming to him too fast, but Capone ignored him. Finally, Collier picked up a sopping bundle and flung it into Capone's face. Before the guards could stop the fight, Capone had blackened both of his attacker's eyes. Both men spent eight days in the hole for the altercation.

Another strike, this time a general one, took place without Capone in January of the following year. The immediate provocation was the death of a prisoner with a stomach ulcer, whom Johnston had refused medical treatment because he thought he was pretending to be sick. Capone stuck to his post again, once more incurring the wrath of the strikers. But it was not cowardice that kept him from striking; he knew the odds and knew there was nothing to be gained by going up against the guards. He asked to be excused from work and was allowed to remain in his cell until the strike ended. Capone was not alone in his idea. Nearly all of the prison's high-profile inmates—felons like Doc Barker, George "Machine Gun" Kelly, kidnappers Albert Bates and Harvey Bailey and train robber and escape artist Roy Gardner—shared Capone's prudence and likewise incurred the dislike and hatred of the strikers.

Capone's request was granted. On his first day back at work, the strikers having been starved into submission, an unknown person hurled a sash weight at his head. Roy Gardner saw it coming and threw himself at Capone, shoving the other man aside. The weight still managed to strike Capone's arm, inflicting a deep cut. After that, he was transferred to the bathhouse cleaning crew. The bathhouse adjoined the barbershop. On the morning of June 23, five months after the second strike, Jim Lucas, a Texas bank robber, reported for his monthly haircut. When he left, he grabbed a pair of scissors, slipped up behind Capone, who was mopping the bathhouse floor, and drove the blades into his back. Capone recovered after a week in the hospital and Lucas went to the hole.

After this incident, a San Francisco lawyer, representing Mae Capone, appealed to the attorney general to have Capone incarcerated somewhere else, but all of his requests were refused. Other attempts followed to kill or maim Capone. His friends exposed a plan to doctor his coffee with lye one morning, and on his way to the dentist, he was jumped and almost strangled before he broke his attacker's hold and knocked the man down.

The attempts on Capone's life, the days of silence, trips to the hole, the grinding daily routine and likely what was, by now, an advanced case of syphilis began to take their toll on Capone. Eventually, he stopped going into the recreation yard and practiced his banjo instead. Once practice was over, he returned immediately to his cell, avoiding all of the inmates except for a few of his closest friends. Occasionally, guards reported that he would refuse to leave his cell to go to the mess hall and eat. They would often find him crouched down in the corner of his cell like an animal. On other occasions, he would mumble to himself, babble in baby talk or simply sit on his bed and strum little tunes on the banjo. Years later, another inmate recalled that Capone would sometimes stay in his cell and make his bunk over and over again.

When the guards decided that the weather was cold enough for the inmates to wear their pea coats, they indicated the decision with three blasts of a whistle. The morning of February 5, 1938, started off unseasonably warm and no whistle blew. Capone nevertheless put on his pea coat. For a year, he had been on library duty, delivering and collecting books and magazines. Alvin Karpis, who occupied the second cell to the left of Capone and always followed him in the line to the mess hall, had a magazine to return, and he tossed it into Capone's cell as he passed it. Seeing Capone standing there in his winter coat, including a cap and gloves, he called to him that he didn't need his jacket that day. Capone seemed to neither hear nor recognize him. He simply stood there, staring vacantly into space.

Capone failed to fall into line when ordered to do so, a breach of discipline ordinarily punished by a trip to the hole, but the guards sensed that something was seriously wrong and watched without disturbing him. He finally left his cell and entered the mess hall last in line. A thread of drool dripped down his chin. As he moved mechanically toward the steam table, a deputy warden, Ernest Miller, spoke to him quietly and patted his arm. Capone grinned strangely and for some reason pointed out the window. Then, suddenly, he started to choke and retch. Miller led him to a locked gate across the hall and called to the guard on the other side to unlock it. They helped Capone up a flight of stairs to the hospital ward.

To the prison physician, and to the consulting psychiatrist he sent for, Capone's symptoms suggested damage to the central nervous system characteristic of advanced syphilis. When Capone, after a return to lucidity, understood this, he finally agreed to the spinal puncture and the other tests that he had refused in Atlanta. The fluid was rushed to the Marine Hospital in San Francisco for analysis. Warden Johnston later stopped by his bed to ask him what had happened to him that morning. Capone replied, "I dunno, they tell me that I acted like I was a little whacky."

The report from the Marine Hospital confirmed the doctor's diagnosis. Word of it reached the press, and newspapers from coast to coast painted a picture of Capone as a man driven insane by the horrors of Alcatraz. Mae Capone pleaded with Warden Johnston by telephone, imploring him to free her husband, an act that was far beyond his power. The hardened warden must have taken some pity on the former "King of Chicago." Capone was never returned to the cellblock and spent the remainder of his sentence in the hospital ward, subjected to injections of arsphenamine, shock treatments and induced fever. His disease was slowed down but not stopped. He alternated between lucidity and confusion, coming to the brink of total insanity. He spent most of his time sitting by himself, plucking at the strings of his banjo, unaware of his surroundings.

Capone's last day on Alcatraz was January 6, 1939. He was then transferred to the new federal prison at Terminal Island near Los Angeles. The following November, Capone was transferred to the U.S. Penitentiary at Lewisburg, Pennsylvania. He arrived on November 16 and was met by Ralph and Mae Capone, who drove him to Baltimore's Union Hospital. Until spring, he lived with Mae in Baltimore as an outpatient of the hospital under the care of Dr. Joseph Moore, a syphilis specialist.

Capone's final years were lived out on his estate near Miami. No outsiders were ever allowed into the compound or near Al because, Ralph cautioned, in his foggy mental state, he might talk about the organization. Probably because Capone slept so badly, the household kept strange hours. They often retired about 10:00 p.m. and were up again by 3:00 a.m. Most of the day was spent next to the pool. Capone, wearing pajamas and a dressing gown, would spend hours on the dock, smoking cigars and holding a fishing rod. Occasionally, he would hit a tennis ball over the net that had been strung across the yard. He hated to be alone and always wanted people around him, provided that he recognized them as trusted friends. He enjoyed playing gin rummy and pinochle, but the mental effort was usually too much for him and his friends let him win.

On January 19, 1947, at just after 4:00 a.m., Capone collapsed from a brain hemorrhage. The newspapers announced that Capone was dead, but he rallied and doctors pronounced him out of danger. The following week, though, he developed bronchial pneumonia and reporters began to gather outside the compound's locked gates. As the hot day wore on, Ralph let them inside and offered them iced beer. On Saturday evening, January 25, Capone died at the age of forty-eight.

Capone's body was returned to Chicago for burial. He was buried on a cold winter's day in Mount Olivet Cemetery, sharing a black granite marker with his father, Gabriel, and his brother, Frank, who had been killed by police in Cicero. This was no typical "gangland funeral"; it was a simple affair with only family and Al's closest remaining friends in attendance. When

Capone spent most of his final days in seclusion at his Miami home, fishing and rarely changing out of his bathrobe. His mind was shattered by illness, and the man who once ruled Chicago was a shadow of his former self. *Courtesy of the* Chicago Daily News.

Capone's mother, Teresa, died in 1952, Capone's body was moved to Mount Carmel Cemetery, where he now lies in the same burial ground with Dion O'Banion, Hymie Weiss and the Genna brothers.

It was a quiet end to the life of the man who once ruled Chicago.

The Murder Castle

In 1893, Chicago became home to the spectacular World's Columbian Exposition, which celebrated the anniversary of Columbus's discovery of America. It was a boom time for the city, and hundreds of thousands of people came from all over the country to attend. Unfortunately, though, the list of those "gone missing" at the end of the fair was extensive, and as the police later tried to track down where these people had vanished to, the trail often turned cold on the South Side of the city. Everything was not as shiny and beautiful as the advertising for the Exposition's "White City" would have had everyone believe, for "a devil" who became known as America's first real serial killer was alive and well on the city's South Side, luring visitors to his "hotel," where scores of them vanished without a trace—never to be seen again.

Herman Mudgett, who went by the name H.H. Holmes, was born in 1860 in Gilmanton, New Hampshire, where his father was a wealthy and respected citizen and the local postmaster for nearly twenty-five years. In 1878, Holmes married Clara Lovering, and that same year he began studying medicine at a small college in Burlington, Vermont. He paid his tuition with a tidy legacy that his wife had inherited. Even as a student, though, Holmes began to dabble in crime. Using cadavers stolen from the morgue, he would stage accidents in which the corpses "died" so that he could collect on insurance policies that he had taken out. Eventually, Holmes dropped out of sight, abandoning his wife and infant son. Clara returned to New Hampshire and never saw her husband again.

Herman Mudgett, alias H.H. Holmes.

In 1885, Holmes turned up in Chicago and opened an office in the North Shore suburb of Wilmette. Holmes had never filed for divorce from Clara Lovering, but this did not stop him from marrying another woman, Myrtle Z. Belknap, whose father, John Belknap, was a wealthy businessman in Wilmette. Although the marriage produced a daughter, Myrtle remained living in Wilmette while Holmes began living in Chicago. Myrtle ended the marriage in 1889.

Shortly after Holmes married Myrtle, he opened another office, this time in downtown Chicago, selling the ABC Copier, a machine for copying documents. He operated from an office on South Dearborn, but the copier was a failure and he vanished again, leaving his creditors with $9,000 in worthless notes.

In 1887, Holmes took over the management of a drugstore in Englewood, on the South Side of the city. The owner of the store conveniently vanished a short time later, and Holmes told the curious that she had sold him the business and left town. She left no forwarding address.

He acquired a large lot across the street from the drugstore and began construction on an enormous edifice that he planned to operate as a hotel for the upcoming Columbian Exposition in 1893. The purchase of the property was financed by an insurance swindle that was aided by an accomplice named Benjamin Pietzel. There are no records of what Holmes decided to call this building, but for generations of police officers, crime enthusiasts and unnerved residents of Englewood, it was known simply by one name—"The Murder Castle."

In 1890, Holmes hired L.L. "Ned" Connor of Davenport, Iowa, as a watchmaker and jeweler for his store. The young man arrived in the city in the company of his wife, Julia, and their daughter, Pearl. The family moved into a small apartment above the store, and soon Julia managed to capture the interest of Holmes. He fired his bookkeeper and hired Julia to take the man's place. Not long after, Connor began to suspect that Holmes was having an affair with his wife. He abandoned his family and went to work for another shop downtown. Holmes took out large insurance policies on Julia and Pearl, naming himself as beneficiary.

Most of Holmes's time was being spent on the construction of his new building. It was an imposing structure of three stories and a basement, with false battlements and wooden bay windows that were covered with sheet iron. There were over sixty rooms in the structure and fifty-one doors that were cut oddly into various walls. Holmes acted as his own architect for the site, and he personally supervised the numerous construction crews, all of whom were quickly hired and fired. He discharged them with great fury and refused to pay their wages. He paid for few of the materials that went into the building. In addition to the eccentric general design, the house was also fitted with trapdoors, hidden staircases, secret passages, rooms without windows, chutes that led into the basement and a staircase that opened out over a steep drop to the alley behind the house.

The first floor of the building contained stores and shops, while the upper floors could be used for spacious living quarters. Holmes also had an office on the second floor, but most of the rooms were to be used for guests—guests who checked in but never checked out. Evidence would later be found to show that Holmes used some of the rooms as "asphyxiation chambers," where his victims were suffocated with gas. All of his "prison rooms" were fitted with alarms that buzzed in Holmes's quarters if a captive attempted to escape.

The castle was completed in 1892, and soon after Holmes announced that he planned to rent out some of the rooms to tourists who would be arriving en masse for the upcoming Columbian Exposition. It is surmised that many of these tourists never returned home after the fair, but no one knows for sure. The list of the "missing" when the fair closed was a long one and, for most, foul play was suspected. How many of them fell prey to Holmes is a mystery, but no fewer than fifty people who were reported to the police as missing were traced to the place. Their trails ended at Holmes's castle.

An advertisement for lodging during the fair was not the only method that Holmes used for procuring victims. A large number of his female victims were lured by classified ads that he placed in small-town newspapers, offering jobs to young ladies. When the applicant arrived and Holmes was convinced that she had told no one of her destination, she would become his prisoner. Holmes placed newspaper ads for marriage as well, describing himself as a wealthy businessman who was searching for a suitable wife. Those who answered this ad often vanished without a trace.

Amazingly, Holmes was able to keep his murder operation a secret for four years. He slaughtered an unknown number of people, mostly women, in the castle. He would later confess to twenty-eight murders, although the actual number of victims is believed to be much higher.

In 1893, Holmes met a young woman named Minnie Williams. He told her that his name was Harry Gordon and that he was a wealthy inventor. Holmes's interest in her had been piqued when he learned that she was the heir to a Texas real estate fortune. She was in Chicago working as an instructor for a private school. It wasn't long before she and Holmes were engaged to be married. This was a turn of events that did not make Julia Connor happy. Not long after the engagement became official, both Julia and Pearl disappeared. When Ned Connor later inquired after them, Holmes explained that they had moved to Michigan. In his later confession, he admitted that Julia had died during a bungled abortion that he had performed on her. He

A photograph of the Murder Castle taken in the early 1930s, before the building was torn down to make room for the post office that is now located at the site. *Courtesy of the Chicago Historical Society.*

had poisoned Pearl. He later admitted that he murdered the woman and her child because of her jealous feelings toward Minnie Williams but added that he would have killed her anyway because he was tired of her.

Minnie Williams lived at the castle for more than a year and knew more about Holmes's crimes than any other person. Besides being partially responsible for the deaths of Julia and Pearl Connor, Minnie was also believed to have instigated the murder of Emily Van Tassel, a young lady who lived on Robey Street. Emily was only seventeen and worked at a candy store on the first floor of the castle. She vanished just one month after her employment at the candy store began.

Minnie also knew about the murder of Emmeline Cigrand, a beautiful young woman who worked as a stenographer at the Keely Institute in Dwight, Illinois. Ben Pietzel went there to take a drunkenness cure and told Holmes of the girl's beauty when he returned to Chicago. Holmes then contacted her and offered her a large salary to work for him in Chicago. She accepted the job and came to the castle—but she never left. Holmes later confessed that he had locked the girl in one of his soundproof rooms and raped her. He stated that he killed her because Minnie Williams objected to his lusting after the attractive young woman.

A visit to Chicago by Minnie's sister, Nannie, may provide more evidence of Minnie's murderous ways and her willingness to go along with Holmes's schemes. In June 1893, Holmes seduced Nannie while she was staying at the castle and had no trouble persuading her to sign over her share of some property in Texas. She disappeared a month later, and according to Holmes, it was Minnie who killed her. When Minnie found out that Nannie had been consorting with Holmes, the two of them got into a heated argument. Minnie hit her sister over the head with a chair and she died; then she and Holmes dropped the body into Lake Michigan.

A short time later, Holmes and Minnie traveled to Denver in the company of another young woman, Georgianna Yoke, who had come to Chicago from Indiana with a "tarnished reputation." On January 17, 1894, Holmes and Georgianna were married at the Vendome Hotel in Denver with Minnie as their witness. After that, the three of them traveled to Texas, where they claimed Minnie's property and arranged a horse swindle. Holmes purchased several railroad cars of horses with counterfeit banknotes. The horses were then shipped to St. Louis and sold. Holmes made off with a fortune, but it would be this swindle that would later destroy him.

The threesome returned to Chicago, and this was the last time that Minnie was ever seen alive. Holmes later claimed that Minnie had fled to Europe after killing her sister, but most likely she was another name on the long list of Holmes's victims.

In July 1894, Holmes was arrested for the first time, not for murder but for one of his schemes: the earlier horse swindle that ended in St. Louis. Georgianna promptly bailed him out, but while in jail, he struck up a conversation with a convicted train robber named Marion Hedgepeth, who was serving a twenty-five-year sentence. Holmes had concocted a plan to bilk an insurance company and offered Hedgepeth a commission in exchange for the name of an attorney who could be trusted. He was directed to Colonel Jeptha Howe, who went along with Holmes's plan of faking his death. When it was all over, the insurance company suspected fraud and refused to pay. Holmes returned to Chicago without pressing the claim and began concocting a new version of the same scheme.

A month later, Holmes, Howe and Ben Pietzel came up with a plan. Pietzel was sent to Philadelphia, where Holmes planned to fake his death and put a burned corpse in Pietzel's place. The scheme went off without a hitch, except that, instead of substituting a corpse for Pietzel's body, Holmes actually killed him. Within days, attorney Jeptha Howe filed a claim with the insurance company, on behalf of Carrie Pietzel, and collected the money. He kept $2,500 and Holmes took the remainder. Howe later gave $500 to Mrs. Pietzel but then took it back, explaining that he would invest it for her.

The only other person who did not get paid was Marion Hedgepeth. Holmes never bothered to contact the train robber again. Hedgepeth brooded over this for a while and then decided to turn Holmes in to the authorities. The police notified the insurance company, which passed on the information to Frank P. Geyer, an insurance investigator. Holmes was eventually arrested in Philadelphia on November 17, 1894.

Holmes was given the choice of being returned to Texas and being hanged as a horse thief or confessing to the insurance scheme that had led to the death of Ben Pietzel. He chose insurance fraud, thinking he would be safe, but his entire maze of crime began to unravel. Frank Geyer was slowly starting to uncover the dark secrets of H.H. Holmes and began trying to discover the fates of the Pietzel children. Their mother had been found but told police that her children had been in Holmes's care. Holmes swore that Minnie Williams had taken the children with her to London, where she planned to open a massage parlor, but Geyer was sure that he was lying. In June 1895, Holmes entered a guilty plea for a single count of insurance fraud, but Geyer expanded his investigation.

Throughout his questioning, Holmes refused to reveal any explanation about what had become of Carrie Pietzel's three children, Howard, Nellie and Alice. Geyer's worst fears soon came to realization. He followed Holmes's trail for eight months through the Midwest and Canada, stopping in each city to investigate the house that Holmes had rented there. In Toronto, he found the bodies of Nellie and Alice Pietzel buried in the backyard of a cottage, and in the Indianapolis suburb of Irvington, he found Howard's charred remains in the stove of a house that Holmes had rented for a week.

As Holmes's crimes came to light, the police began to search his residence in Chicago. None of the officers would ever forget what they found there, and detectives devoted several weeks to searching and making a floor plan of the castle.

The second floor proved to be a labyrinth of narrow, winding passages, with doors that opened to brick walls, hidden stairways, cleverly concealed

Holmes's accomplice Benjamin Pietzel. *Courtesy of Brenda and Beth Pietzel.*

doors, blind hallways, secret panels, hidden passages and a clandestine vault that was only big enough for one person to stand in. The room was alleged to be a homemade "gas chamber," equipped with a chute that would carry a body directly into the basement. The investigators suddenly realized the implications of the iron-plated chamber when they found the single scuffed mark of a woman's footprint on the inside of the door.

In addition to all of the bizarre embellishments to the floor, the second level also held thirty-five guest rooms. Half of them were fitted as ordinary sleeping chambers, and several of the other rooms were without windows and could be made airtight by closing the doors. Others were lined with sheet iron and asbestos, with scorch marks on the walls; fitted with trapdoors that led to smaller rooms beneath; or equipped with lethal gas jets that could be used to suffocate or burn the unsuspecting occupants.

This floor also contained Holmes's private apartment, consisting of a bedroom, a bath and two small chambers that were used as offices. The apartment was located at the front of the building, looking out over Sixty-third Street. In the floor of the bathroom, concealed under a heavy rug, the police found a trapdoor and a stairway that descended to a room about eight feet square. Two doors led off this chamber, one to a stairway that exited out onto the street and the other giving access to the chute that led down to the basement.

The "chamber of horrors" in the basement stunned the men even further. This subterranean chamber was located seven feet below the rest of the building and extended out under the sidewalk in front. Here, they found Holmes's blood-spattered dissecting table, his gleaming surgical instruments, his macabre "laboratory" of torture devices, various jars of poison and even a wooden box that contained a number of female skeletons. A large stove had apparently been used as a crematorium and still contained ash and portions of bone that had not burned in the intense heat. A search of the ashes revealed a watch that had belonged to Minnie Williams, some buttons from a dress and several charred tintype photographs.

Buried in the floor, the police found a huge vat of corrosive acid and two quicklime pits, which were capable of devouring an entire body in a matter of hours. A loose pile of quicklime was also discovered in a small room that had been built into the corner.

Less than two weeks after it was vacated by the police, H.H. Holmes's "Murder Castle" was purchased by a man named A.M. Clark, who planned to open it as a tourist attraction, capitalizing on the sensationalistic press that surrounded the discoveries inside. On August 19, it was ready to admit its first paying customers, but that same night A.M. Clark's get-rich-quick scheme literally went up in smoke.

No one ever found out how the fire got started. Some saw it as an act of divine retribution as God purged Chicago of Holmes's "chamber of horrors." Others suggested that perhaps it had been a resident of Englewood, ashamed of the blemish that the castle had created on the city's reputation. The police, on the other hand, took another view. They suspected that a confederate of Holmes had torched the place to conceal incriminating evidence that the investigators had overlooked.

Whatever the source of the fire, it made short work of the building. At precisely 12:13 a.m., a night watchman at the Western Indiana railroad crossing spotted flames coming through the building's roof. Before he could turn in the alarm, a series of explosions rocked the building, blowing out the windows of the candy shop on the first floor. By the time the first fire engines arrived, the blaze was nearly out of control. A half hour later, the roof collapsed, taking down part of the castle's rear wall. By the time the blaze was extinguished, about an hour and a half after it was first reported, much of the structure had been consumed.

Although the first floor shops sustained only minimal damage, the two upper stories of the building were completely gutted. The new "murder museum" was a blackened shell, and A.M. Clark was out of business for good. Contrary to many stories, the fire did not destroy the castle completely. Even though the second and third floors were sealed off, and their windows boarded over, the first floor remained in operation for many years. A sign shop and a bookstore operated there until the building was sold in 1937. The lot was sold and the building razed in January 1938 to make way for the U.S. Post Office that still stands at the site today.

The trial of Herman Mudgett, aka H.H. Holmes, began in Philadelphia just before Halloween 1895. It only lasted for six days but was one of the most sensational of the century. On November 30, the judge passed a sentence of death. His case was appealed to the Pennsylvania Supreme Court, who affirmed the verdict, and the governor refused to intervene. Holmes was scheduled to die on May 7, 1896, just nine days before his thirty-sixth birthday.

By now, the details of the case had been made public, and people were angry, horrified and fascinated, especially in Chicago, where most of the evil had occurred. Holmes had provided a lurid confession of torture and murder that appeared in newspapers and magazines, providing a litany of depravity that compares with the most insane killers of all time. Even if his story was embellished, the actual evidence of Holmes's crimes ranks him as one of the country's most active murderers.

He remained unrepentant, though, even at the end. Just before his execution, he visited with two Catholic priests in his cell and even took communion with them, although he refused to ask forgiveness for his crimes. He was led from his cell to the gallows and a black hood was placed over his head. The trapdoor opened beneath him and Holmes quickly dropped. His head snapped to the side, but his fingers clenched and his feet danced, causing many spectators to look away. The rope around his neck had pulled so tight that it imbedded itself in his flesh, but his heart continued to beat for nearly fifteen minutes, marking the final excruciating moments in the life of the man some called the "devil incarnate."

The Car Barn Bandits

Depending on your point of view, the "Car Barn Bandits," who wreaked havoc in Chicago in 1903, were either the first or the last of their kind. Some saw them as the first organized crime ring to operate in the city, which would make them a foreshadowing of things to come, while others saw their exploits as something out of a Wild West dime novel, hearkening back to an earlier generation. No matter what they were, they were undoubtedly one of the deadliest gangs to terrify Chicago in the early twentieth century.

The bandits were young men, barely out of their teens, and the gang was made up of Peter Niedermeyer, Gustav Marx, Harvey Van Dine and Emil Roeski. They had all grown up together on the northwest side of the city and all came from good families that offered them love, support and good educations. Somewhere along the line, though, they simply went bad, cultivating a record of robbery and murder that shocked Chicago at the time of their capture.

Their criminal exploits began in the summer of 1903, when they committed a number of robberies, holdups and murders. On July 20, they robbed a bar on Milwaukee Avenue, wounding a saloonkeeper named Peter Gorski. On August 2, they struck again at a bar on West North Avenue and killed the owner, Benjamin La Grosse, and a twenty-one-year-old customer. They committed robbery and murder at Greenberg's Saloon, located at the southwest corner of Addison and Robey Streets (now Damen Avenue), and followed that with another holdup in a tavern at Roscoe Street and Sheffield Avenue. By all accounts, the bandits were having more fun than they had ever had in their lives.

One August night, while they were walking around the city, the gang members noticed some men counting money inside of a railroad car barn. This gave them an idea and they began planning another robbery. On the night of August 30, 1903, Niedermeyer, Marx and Van Dine met on Sixty-third Street on Chicago's South Side and walked over to the City Railway Company car barn, which was located just two blocks away. They found the door unlocked, and they simply walked in and pulled their guns on the startled clerks. They immediately began searching for money. Van Dine smashed open a door with a sledgehammer and stormed into an office. According to Marx, he saw police officers outside and, to hurry things along, fired a few shots into the ceiling. A window was smashed open and Niedermeyer began shooting out of it, aiming for the men who had been spotted outside. They weren't police officers but railroad workers, and in the confusion, a railroad motorman was killed and two cashiers were wounded. Meanwhile, Van Dine had ransacked the office and came out with a bundle of cash under his arm. "I've got enough, boys!" he shouted at his friends, and the bandits fled the scene, running toward Sixtieth Street.

The area seemed deserted, and no one followed them as they strolled down the old midway into Jackson Park, the now abandoned site of the World's Fair of ten years earlier. They roamed the park and the ruins of the exposition until daybreak, and then they divided their loot, which came to $2,250. They took a streetcar downtown and celebrated their success with cigars and a big breakfast. Afterward, they had a grand time reading about their "daring robbery" in the morning editions of the local newspapers. The stories noted that the police had no idea as to the identities of the young robbers.

The next day, the three boys, along with Emil Roeski, spent the afternoon in Humboldt Park, smoking cigars and reading more stories about the robbery. They began to dream of something even more adventurous—robbing trains. After a night at an expensive hotel, they used some of their ill-gotten gain to purchase train tickets to Denver, Colorado, believing that it would be easy to buy dynamite in one of the nearby mining towns. They enjoyed themselves for a few days in Denver and then went to Cripple Creek, where they purchased a bundle of dynamite in a mining supply store. They quickly returned to Chicago, still making big plans.

The robbery turned out to be a bust. They packed about fifty pounds of dynamite near the Northwestern Tracks in Jefferson Park and made plans to stop the train. Roeski waved a red flag at the train as it approached, but the engine never even slowed down. Angry, he pulled out his revolver and fired a shot at the train, which finally stopped it. Unfortunately, it stopped too far away from the dynamite for them to rob it according to plan, and the bandits ran away.

The failed robbery attempt frightened the young robbers and they became increasingly paranoid. Van Dine spent three days at his window with a rifle, waiting for the police to come. He finally calmed down, but his paranoia, as it turned out, was not unjustified. The police were looking for them—not for the failed train robbery, but for their earlier robberies. The methods the young men had employed in various tavern holdups caused the police to suspect that they were the Car Barn Bandits.

In spite of the fact that they knew the police were looking for them, the bandits boldly went out drinking, paying big tips and brandishing their revolvers. The police tracked down Gustav Marx first and came to arrest him at Greenberg's Saloon, which he and his friends had robbed earlier that summer. Police Detective John Quinn entered the front door and Detective William Blaul slipped in through a side entrance. When Marx saw the officer walk in, he quickly pulled his gun. Out of the corner of his eye, he saw Quinn come through the front door and he turned and shot him. As Quinn fell lifeless to the floor, Blaul opened fire and wounded Marx in the arm. Blaul grabbed the bandit, who tried to flee, and dragged him across the room to a telephone. He called the station house for backup as Marx begged him to "Kill me! Kill me now!"

But Detective Blaul didn't kill him. Instead, he took him to the police station and locked him up. Marx fumed in his cell for a while, and when his friends didn't show up to bust him out, as they had planned to do in the event that any of them were captured, he angrily decided to confess every detail of the Car Barn Bandits' crimes. He spilled his guts about twenty robberies and six murders—seven, counting the shooting of Detective Quinn.

The police began a massive manhunt for Niedermeyer, Van Dine and Roeski. Word came in that a general store owner had spotted them in the town of Clark Station, and it was realized that they planned to make their escape into the wilds of the Indiana Dunes. Eight detectives were dispatched on their trail, but the men quickly became lost in the tangle of unmarked roads, sand dunes and forests. They followed several leads but became lost over and over again. One of the wagons in which they were traveling overturned in the sand, injuring a few of the detectives. Eventually, late in the night, they found a dugout in the dunes that was located about two hundred feet from the Baltimore & Ohio Railroad tracks and three miles from the closest town. The hideout was empty, but some leftover sausage links found inside showed that it had recently been in use. This meant that the bandits were still somewhere nearby.

The detectives stayed the night in a barn near Edgemoor, Indiana. When daylight came, the farmer's wife brought them coffee, and they went out into the November snow. Later that morning, they found another railroad dugout, similar to the one they had discovered the night before. The dugout was the cellar of a railroad telegrapher's home that had burned down years before, and it was surrounded by fresh footprints in the snow. However, the entrance to the dugout had been covered with boards, and the detectives had trouble finding another way inside. After some time, an old staircase was discovered, and the detectives took up position around it, revolvers in hand, and shouted for the bandits to come out.

A reply was heard from the darkness below. "We'll come out when you carry us out!" a voice cried, and the sound was followed by several gunshots.

The detectives fired their guns down the staircase, and after a pause, Niedermeyer's face appeared at the bottom of the steps. The detectives

Detectives investigate one of the railroad dugouts where the Car Barn Bandits hid in the Indiana Dunes. *Courtesy of the* Chicago Daily News.

assumed that he was surrendering, but instead, he pulled out two guns, fired manically at them and then ducked out of sight. The exchange of gunfire continued, with dire results for the policemen. Officer Joseph R. Driscoll was shot in the abdomen and Officer Matthew Zimmer was wounded in the arm. Harvey Van Dine came out of the dugout long enough to shoot Zimmer again, this time in the head.

As the police officers pulled back, the bandits made a daring escape from the dugout. They ran away on foot, firing at the detectives as they hurried toward the woods. Niedermeyer was hit once in the neck as he ran down a hill into a ravine but managed to get back up and keep running with the others. The bandits escaped while the detectives wired for reinforcements and tried to tend to their wounded comrades. The officers were able to flag down a passing train, and the wounded men were put onboard and taken to a hospital. Officer Driscoll died a few days later.

Fifty police officers with repeating rifles were rushed to the scene onboard a special train. They followed the tracks south, stopping to examine the deserted dugout where the bandits had been found. The room was well stocked with food and ammunition and outfitted with bunk beds.

The original detectives, now five in number, followed the bandits' trail through the snow, passing a brakemen's cottage that the outlaws had tried to break into and failed. As they followed the footprints and occasional spatters of blood in the snow, they were startled by and opened fire on what turned out to be nothing but Niedermeyer's overcoat, which he had strung up in some tree branches as a decoy. One set of tracks, Roeski's, led into a cornfield and the others continued south. Roeski, who had been wounded badly in the gun battle, was captured in the cornfield later that day.

Niedermeyer and Van Dine made it to the town of East Tolleston, four miles from the dugout. There, they found a Pennsylvania Railroad gravel train sitting on the tracks, preparing to leave. The engineer had gone to get dinner for the fireman, Albert Coffey, who was still in the cab. The bandits climbed into the cab and put a revolver to the fireman's head. A brakeman, L.J. Sovea, thought the bandits were rail yard drunks, and he jumped up and grabbed Niedermeyer by the wrist. During a struggle, Sovea was shot in the face and his lifeless body was dumped on the side of the tracks.

The bandits forced Coffey to start the engine, and he took them two miles to the town of Liverpool, where a locked switch prevented him from going any farther. Niedermeyer and Van Dine made him back up almost a half mile and then they jumped out of the cab and ran across the prairie.

Meanwhile, posses made up of farmers and police officers formed in East Tolleston to pursue the men. Liverpool had been warned about them by telegraph and sent out a posse of its own. The Liverpool posse tracked down the fleeing robbers as they ran toward a cornfield and opened fire on them—with shotguns filled with birdshot. Niedermeyer and Van Dine were both hit in the face, but the wounds were far from fatal. Nevertheless, they surrendered. They were taken back to Liverpool and then sent back to Chicago. Indiana governor Winfield Durbin promptly issued a statement: "I congratulate the authorities on the capture. Chicago can keep the prisoners—Indiana doesn't want them."

The six-month crime spree of the Car Barn Bandits had finally ended. The laughing young men were quick to admit to their robberies and murders, and all of them were soon charged with murder and put on trial. The bandits confessed not only to crimes in Chicago but also to other holdups around the country. They wanted to make sure that everyone knew just who had committed the crimes. Niedermeyer kept track of the crimes that offered rewards and demanded that his mother be given the money since he had provided the information. The confessions told of daring lives of crime that became the stuff of short-lived legend. It was revealed that they had robbed 114 people and killed 8 in just sixty days. The case captured the attention of the public, and newspapers around the country sent reporters to Chicago to cover the trial.

Nothing could be done to save the young bandits at their trials since they had already confessed to everything they had done. Niedermeyer, Van Dine and Marx were tried together, and Roeski was given a separate trial since he wasn't present at the car barn robbery. Attempts were made to show that the boys were "victims of society" and that insanity ran in Van Dine's family, but the jury wasn't fooled. The first three defendants were found guilty and sentenced to hang.

At Roeski's trial, Marx swore that he, not Roeski, had killed nineteen-year-old Otto Bauder on July 9 at Ernest Spire's tavern on North Ashland Avenue, a crime for which Roeski was accused. However, on April 20, 1904, Roeski was found guilty of murder, but the jury decided to spare his life since there was still some question as to whether he had pulled the trigger during Bauder's murder. He was taken away to Joliet Prison and his friends were scheduled to hang two days later.

The bandits were housed at the Cook County Jail before their executions. Niedermeyer attempted suicide by trying to cut his wrist with a lead

Car Barn Bandit Gustav Marx waits for his execution at the Cook County Jail. *Courtesy of the* Chicago Daily News.

pencil and by swallowing the sulfur tips of matches. On the day before the hangings, though, the three condemned men sat quietly, talking and smoking with their jailers.

Outside the jail, a crowd that numbered almost one thousand gathered to wait for news about what was happening inside. A detail of one hundred police officers surrounded the jail to keep the onlookers in line and to prevent them from loitering on Dearborn Street.

Niedermeyer was scheduled to be the first to die, insisting to anyone who would listen that he would "die game." But when the time actually came to go to the gallows, his courage gave way and he nearly fainted. The guards placed him on a gurney and wheeled him to the scaffold. Too weak to stand, he was strapped to a chair and a hood was placed over his head. The trap was sprung and the bandit dropped to his death, still seated in the chair. The shroud fell off, and the assembled crowd was shocked by the gruesome sight

A crowd gathered on the street outside of the jail, awaiting word of the Car Barn Bandits' executions. The young criminals created a sensation in Chicago in the early 1900s. *Courtesy of the* Chicago Daily News.

of his face as he strangled to death. His neck was broken, but it took him nearly twenty minutes to die.

Marx was brought out next. He was praying and holding a crucifix as he walked to the gallows. He continued to pray as the shroud was placed over his face and the rope slipped around his neck. He died instantly.

Van Dine also prayed as the trap was opened and, like Marx, he died when his neck snapped.

For years, the Car Barn Bandits were hailed as the most famous criminal gang in Chicago history. On numerous occasions, gangs of amateur bandits who idolized them were captured, sometimes while lurking in the bandits' old hideouts. Eventually, though, they faded into history, and by the latter part of the twentieth century, they were almost completely forgotten.

The Mysterious Death of Marshall Field Jr.

If there could be only one name to epitomize the rise of business in Chicago, it would be that of Marshall Field. Dubbed the "Merchant Prince," he began creating an empire in the city before the Civil War and went on to found the world's first department store in downtown Chicago. Both glorified and feared, Marshall Field was considered a Chicago icon and one of the richest men in the world in his day, with an estate of more than $140 million. He made a fortune from the city of Chicago but gave much of it back, including the lakefront museum that was established and named in his honor. He also largely founded the Art Institute and laid the groundwork for the University of Chicago.

But despite all of his achievements, a single event occurred in 1905 that would both shorten his life and overshadow many of his accomplishments. The death of his son, Marshall Field Jr., under mysterious circumstances not only sent Field to an early grave but also created one of the great unsolved mysteries of Chicago history.

Marshall Field came to Chicago in 1856 and went to work as a clerk in a dry goods store with a salary of $400 per year, half of which he saved. A pioneer of new merchandising methods, he went on to coin the ultimate customer service slogan of "Give the Lady What She Wants." He and a partner, Levi Z. Leiter, purchased Potter Palmer's store in 1865 and it became Marshall Field and Company. Even before becoming the premier dry goods merchant in the country, though, he looked for other ways to make money and discovered real estate investment. He was known for being a serious, mild-looking man and was well liked, even though he never praised his

Chicago's "Merchant Prince," Marshall Field.

employees and paid them low wages—never a cent more than he had agreed to pay them, no matter how well they performed. Thanks to this, he did not keep partners for long. At each year's end, he held a dinner in his house for partners and members of the upper management. Over after-dinner brandy, he would make simple announcements to the assembled group as to which of them would not be celebrating the holidays with the company the following year. If an employee had not measured up, he would no longer be required by Marshall Field and Company.

In 1876, Field constructed a luxurious mansion with a prestigious address at 1905 South Prairie Avenue. The house cost over $2 million to build and was the first home in Chicago to have electric lights. Field lived there with his wife, the former Nannie Scott of Ironton, Ohio, and she became known as the social queen of the city. In their magnificent home, the Fields reared their son, Marshall Field Jr., and their daughter, Ethel. The family entertained both famous and infamous American and European personages and held many notable parties and balls. Perhaps the most noted event was staged in January 1886, when a party was held in honor of the two Field children. More than five hundred guests were present, and as Gilbert and Sullivan's operetta *Mikado* was then all the rage in the fashionable world, the Field event was designated a "Mikado Ball." Wealthy children and their parents attended the party in colorful Japanese costumes, and their carriages passed beneath special calcium lights that had been erected for the evening. The ball was said to have cost $75,000 and it was talked about for years afterward.

But not everything connected to the Marshall Field family was bright and filled with joy, and the Mikado Ball was certainly not the only thing spoken of in the city for years after it took place.

In 1890, Marshall Field Jr. married a young woman named Albertine Huck and, with his father's help, purchased a Prairie Avenue home just a few doors down from the family mansion. The house, located at 1919 South Prairie Avenue, had been known in the neighborhood as the William H. Murray House, built in 1884. The younger Field purchased the house, with his father's assistance, for $65,000.

The Fields lived happily in the house for a number of years, entertaining and welcoming only the best people on the Chicago social register. However, tragedy occurred at the Field mansion on November 22, 1905. Just before dinner that evening, Marshall Field Jr. fired a bullet into his left side while he was seated in his dressing room. The shot would eventually prove to be fatal. According to the newspapers the following morning, the gunshot had been a tragic accident. Field had been examining a loaded revolver in anticipation of an upcoming hunting trip to Wisconsin when the gun went off. It had accidentally discharged and the bullet lodged in his side, piercing his liver. Field

The home of Marshall Field Jr. in the Prairie Avenue Historic District today.

was rushed to Mercy Hospital, where he lingered at death's door for several days. His parents, when notified of the shooting, rushed back to Chicago.

The police were summoned to the house, and the servants were closely questioned, but no one had witnessed the shooting. Mrs. Field had been away for the afternoon. The parents of the critically wounded man were vacationing in New York at the time. Satisfied with the "cleaning the gun" story, the police looked no further into the incident.

Marshall Field Jr. died on November 27, 1905. Although he initially showed signs of improvement, Field weakened with a high fever and then finally succumbed to his wound during the late afternoon hours. The *Chicago Daily News* reported:

> *Kneeling beside his death bed in Mercy Hospital, holding his left hand in both of hers, was his wife. His father stood at the foot of the bed, his face wet with tears. Mr. Field passed away quietly, holding to his lips a crucifix.*

It was said that Albertine collapsed in hysterics after her husband's death and threw her arms around her father-in-law, who escorted her to his carriage and home.

A private wake was held in the house at 1919 South Prairie Avenue, where Field had been shot just days before. He was buried in a lavish ceremony at Graceland Cemetery on the city's North Side and was soon joined there by his father. On January 16, 1906, the "Merchant Prince," still mourning his son, died from complications of pneumonia and old age.

His death brought an end to a chapter in Chicago history and created a mystery that few would have talked about while the elder Field was still alive.

The city was humming with rumors and whispers after the death of the Fields. Police detectives may have accepted "accidental discharge" as a cause of death for the younger Field, but many reporters and members of the general public were not so quick to do so. While Field was lingering near death at Mercy Hospital, reporters and photographers swarmed the hallways of the place, taking photographs and looking for information from doctors, nurses, cops and even distressed family members. The eighty-seven-year-old Marshall Field took to fending them off with his walking stick.

Those reporters were the first to begin looking into the rumors that implied that the younger Field was not the family man that his friends, family and colleagues made him out to be. After his death, he was eulogized in the newspapers by his friends and colleagues as a man of "gentle refinements, possessing a quiet and retiring disposition." They spoke of his Harvard education, his enthusiasm for sports and the great outdoors and his abiding love for his wife and children. This was the man presented to the public, but stories claimed that he was a much different person in his private life.

The rumors stated that Field had not been shot in his dressing room but in one of Chicago's most fashionable brothels (the Everleigh Club was usually mentioned). The stories varied, stating that he had either been involved in an altercation in the brothel and was shot by another customer or that he was shot by one of the prostitutes when he became violent with her. Regardless, his body was then smuggled home to avoid scandal for the Field family. He was later found in his room and was said to have had an accident while cleaning his gun. This story spread rapidly, but if there was any evidence of this having actually occurred, it vanished many years ago.

And this was not the only story that circulated in Chicago about Field's death. The other rumor was even more scandalous and, had it been widely believed, would have been even more damaging to the reputation of the Field family. This rumor claimed that Field had not been killed by accident. It said that he had shot himself while attempting suicide. The incident was covered up as an accident in order to conceal the reason that Field took his own life.

According to the story, he was driven to suicide after receiving news that his wife was having an affair. This would have been shocking enough, but the story went on to say that the man she had been having an affair with was none other than Marshall Field himself, her husband's father. Enraged and despondent, Marshall Field Jr. committed suicide rather than face the betrayal by his wife and father. Of course, absolutely no evidence of the affair was ever presented. It was a story that widely circulated, however, and there are many who maintain that the story is true to this day.

No matter what the police believed, the circumstances of Field's death were definitely strange, and the shooting left a number of questions in its wake. For instance, why was Field checking his gun in his dressing room? Why was this experienced outdoorsman "checking" a loaded gun? If he were preparing for a hunting trip, why would he be worried about his pistol?

Unfortunately, too much time has passed for any of these questions to ever be answered, leaving behind a Chicago mystery that will never be solved.

"IL DIAVOLO"

One of the most savage, and most feared, underworld figures in Chicago history was a man named Salvatore Cardinelli, alias Sam Cardinella, who was better known as "Il Diavolo." When Cardinella went to the gallows in April 1921, he broke down in hysterics and had to be tied to a chair, just like Car Barn Bandit Peter Niedermeyer. In Cardinella's case, the emotional scene was a ruse. He had planned every detail of his hysterics on the gallows, and for years rumors claimed that the gangster had only played dead, and had, in fact, escaped with his life. The truth, though, according to eyewitnesses, was even stranger—all of Cardinella's theatrics were performed so that his body could later be brought back to life!

Cardinella's infamy began in the early days of Prohibition. The South Side gang that he created was known for being more ferocious and bloodthirsty than any of the mobsters whose fame still lingers today. Like O'Banion, Torrio and Capone, Cardinella got his start as a criminal in the 1910s. He became involved with the Black Hand, an organized group of extortionists who preyed on wealthy Italian immigrants, demanding money to prevent death and violence. Cardinella earned his nickname of Il Diavolo, Italian for "the Devil," during this time. He was a terrifying figure to the Italian immigrants of the day and even most gangsters were afraid of him and his gang. The police referred to them as a "murder clique," and some reports even compared them to "Hindu thugs," referring to the assassins that operated in India during the nineteenth century.

Cardinella's base of operations was a poolroom in the 200 block of Twenty-second Street, which is now West Cermak Road. The poolroom

Sam Cardinella, otherwise known as "Il Diavolo," was the scourge of Chicago's South Side in the early years of Prohibition. *Courtesy of Adam Selzer.*

was dubbed a "school for crime." Cardinella lured boys off the streets and taught them to pick pockets and commit robberies, just like a villain from a Charles Dickens novel.

One of his recruits was a young man named Nicholas Viana. Viana often saw boys of his own age hanging out in the pool hall as he walked home from choir practice each afternoon, and one day he finally went inside to see what was going on. Soon, he was a full-fledged member of the gang and was taking in the advice that Cardinella was offering to his aspiring thieves and killers. He warned them to never trust a woman, not even their own mothers. He also warned against bragging about their crimes, for it was better to stay away from the notice of local police officers. He sent them out to commit robberies and other violent crimes, taking the largest portion of their loot for himself. He was doing them a service, he explained. He even held onto their guns for them when they were not needed and sternly warned them never to rat out other members of the gang. Those who became informers were killed.

Cardinella planned the gang's crimes in great detail, leaving no clues or common methods of operation that would allow the police to track them. Only those in the underworld even knew that the gang existed, and few of those men knew the true identity of the feared Il Diavolo. Even his family believed that Cardinella was nothing more than the owner of a poolroom.

The police would never put all of the pieces of Cardinella's operation together, but they at least discovered the gang's existence after the murder of Andrew Browman in his tavern at 447 West Twenty-second Street, only two blocks from Cardinella's poolroom. Seven young men walked into the saloon one afternoon and began shooting everything in sight. They emptied the till and vanished. However, a passerby wrote down the license plate number of the getaway car, and this led police to Santo Orlando, who may have been the first gang member to talk. The police kept him in custody for three days and then let him go. It was rumored that he was released after giving information about the gang's operations.

When Orlando disappeared a short time later, Cardinella told the others involved in the robbery that he had smuggled the man out of town, dressed as a woman. Because this had cost him quite a lot of money, he was keeping the boys' share of the tavern robbery. However, he told them, he knew of a carpenter they could rob and get some of the money back for themselves. He gave them a stiletto and told them to use the knife on the man until he revealed where his money was hidden.

The robbery of the carpenter never happened, and it's believed that the boys suspected Cardinella of setting them up. A short time later, Santo Orlando's body was found in the canal, full of bullet holes. Cardinella's bandits knew that he must have talked, and they realized that their boss had tried to get them out of the way so that the tavern robbery could not be traced back to him. Furious at the death of their friend, and by what they saw as Cardinella's betrayal, his gang began to turn against him.

A short time later, as the police were slowly gathering evidence against the gang, a group of boys stormed into a poolroom on Sixty-third Street and robbed the place, killing one man before they left. They made a fatal mistake during the robbery. As they searched everyone in the poolroom for valuables, they passed over Thomas Errico, a gang member who had been sent into the place as an advance man, posing as a regular customer. Several of the real patrons took note of this and told the police about it during the investigation that followed.

Errico was arrested and began providing information to the police. He told the detectives that he belonged to a highly organized gang of thieves and murderers and that he had been involved in more holdups than he could remember. He apparently spilled plenty of details about the crimes because soon after his arrest, sixteen officers raided a poolroom run by Frank Campioni, one of Cardinella's gang members. A number of bandits were arrested, and once behind bars, they began to talk.

All of them gave information about Cardinella, who they felt double-crossed them every chance he got. They confessed to scores of crimes, including at least four murders, and while they doomed Cardinella, they also sealed their own fates. The police announced the greatest victory against organized crime in Chicago since the capture of the Car Barn Bandits and revealed that more than 250 open cases had now been closed.

Cardinella was soon in custody, along with about two dozen of his men, and he became one of fifteen gang members sentenced to death. About half of them were eventually hanged, including Nicholas "the Choir Boy" Viana, who was believed to have killed fifteen men by the time he was eighteen. He was hanged on December 10, 1919—his nineteenth birthday. Viana was the youngest and one of the fiercest members of the gang. Despite the number of homicides he committed, the murder that actually sent him to the gallows was that of Albert Kubleanzo, whose death netted Viana and other members of the gang about $6.50 each.

Three others were sentenced to die on the same day as Cardinella. They were Joe Constanza, Sam Ferrara and Antonio "the Rooster" Lopez. The latter earned his nickname in prison due to his nervous tendency to imitate a rooster, which he also did several times at his trial. While "the Rooster" kept up his crowing in prison, Cardinella became moody and despondent. His dark demeanor bothered the guards and prison officials. Dr. Francis W. McNamara, the jail's chief physician, told the *Chicago Tribune*, "If I were a superstitious man, I would say that Cardinella himself seemed to evoke the spirit of Satanism." He began to refuse to eat and was hostile to the guards, pacing endlessly in his cell. Rumors went around that he had bribed prison officials and a plan was being hatched to get him out of jail. As the day of his execution approached, McNamara claimed there was a "sense of ill omen, of menace, of mysterious evil" in the air.

On the night before his execution, Cardinella was allowed to visit with his wife and six children. He wept openly, destroying the tough demeanor that he had established. He spoke with them in Sicilian, a language that none of the guards could understand, but they did overhear one word that they recognized: "Viana." No one could guess why Cardinella would be talking about the former gang member Nicholas Viana, who had gone to the gallows himself months before.

Cardinella was taken to the death cell that night, but he refused to sleep. Most prisoners on their last night chatted with the guards, smoked, drank coffee or tried to find ways to distract themselves, but Cardinella only paced in gloomy silence. He was scheduled to be the first to die on April 15, 1921, and the other three men, who shared the death cell with him, would hang a half hour later.

Constanza and Ferrara seemed depressed but not angry. Lopez, however, seemed to be in a fine mood. When he was asked if he had any requests, he said that he did, stuck his head out of the death cell and let out a fine rooster's crow. Cheering was heard from all corners of the jail, and he vowed to let out another "cock-a-doodle-doo" on the gallows. But this didn't happen. A couple of hours later, Lopez was granted a stay of execution, and he crowed in triumph as he was taken out of the death cell. He was eventually hanged four months later, but whether he crowed as the rope was being place around his neck was not recorded.

Cardinella, of course, did not earn a reprieve, but he did manage to delay his execution by one hour. He argued that he had been sentenced before Daylight Saving Time, and the extra hour might mean a last-minute call from the governor. He was granted the extra hour, but the governor never called.

As was the custom, Cardinella had been offered whatever he wanted to eat for his last meal, but he turned down the offer. He appeared to be weak as he carried out the motions of a religious service. His constant refusal to eat had caused him to lose a tremendous amount of weight, perhaps as much as forty pounds.

Cardinella suffered an emotional breakdown when the mandate for his execution arrived. He threw himself at the feet of his priest, crying in misery. He was unable to stand up, and the guards were forced to pick him up, tie him to a chair and then carry the chair to the scaffold. He refused to stand on the gallows. No one was sure if he was unable to do so or was simply being difficult, so they left him seated and placed the rope around his neck. A minute later, the trapdoor was opened and Cardinella dropped to his death, chair and all. He strangled to death in six minutes. The body was untied and taken to an ambulance in the jail yard, which was there on the order of the condemned man's friends and family.

As the body was placed in the ambulance, guards saw a woman in a nurse's uniform and a man who looked more like a doctor than an undertaker's assistant. One of the men walked back into the jail and noted that it seemed like an odd group in the ambulance. This comment, along with talk of Cardinella's mention of Nicholas Viana on the previous night, sparked a memory for several of the prison staff. They recalled that when Viana's body was taken out, he was also placed in an ambulance that was staffed by a doctor and a nurse.

The warden suspected that something was amiss, and he delayed the ambulance carrying Cardinella's remains in the jail yard for an hour while the other two men were hanged. He then ordered Cardinella's body removed from the ambulance and placed in the funeral car that was going to the morgue. When the doors to the ambulance were opened again, guards saw the woman in the nurse's outfit rubbing Cardinella's lifeless wrists, cheeks and neck. The man dressed as a doctor was holding a hypodermic needle, injecting something into his chest. Inside of the ambulance was a rubber mattress filled with hot water, an oxygen tank and an electrical battery—all things that, theoretically, could have been used to bring the gangster back to life!

It was believed that Cardinella's demeanor in prison was all an act, performed to increase his chances of being resurrected. By refusing to eat, he lost a great deal of weight, meaning that the fall was less likely to break his neck. His "nervous collapse" meant that he would be tied to a chair, causing him to drop a shorter distance when the trap was sprung. The lesser weight and the shorter fall caused Cardinella to strangle to death instead of being killed by a broken neck. Rumors began to circulate that Cardinella had performed the greatest trick in the prison's history: he had been brought back from the dead and could not be hanged again since the sentence had already been carried out. Dr. McNamara was dispatched to the morgue, where he ran tests on the body to make sure that any further attempts to bring the gang leader back to life would be fruitless.

Cardinella was now definitely dead; however, the physician believed that Cardinella might have been saved if the ambulance had not been held up in the jail yard for that additional hour.

But where did Nicholas "the Choir Boy" Viana fit into the story?

According to stories that were later heard by Dr. McNamara, Cardinella had tested his theory that a hanged man could be brought back to life on Viana several months before. At the time of his execution, Viana's corpse was taken by ambulance to a place where stimulants, hot water and electricity were used to resurrect him. He was allowed to die on the operating table, though, because the plan had not been carried out to revive him, only to see if it could be done again for Cardinella four month later.

Could Cardinella have been resurrected? Dr. McNamara, who shared what he witnessed in April 1921 with a *Chicago Tribune* reporter fifteen years later, certainly believed that it was possible.

CHICAGO'S "THRILL KILLERS"

On an afternoon in May 1924, sons of two of Chicago's wealthiest and most illustrious families drove to the Harvard School on the city's South Side and kidnapped a young boy named Bobby Franks. Their plan was to carry out the "perfect murder." It was a scheme so devious that only two men of superior intellect, such as their own, could accomplish it. These two men were Richard Loeb and Nathan Leopold. They were the privileged heirs of well-known Chicago families who had embarked on a life of crime for fun and for the pure thrill of it. They were also a pair of deviants who considered themselves to be "brilliant"—a claim that would later lead to their downfall.

Nathan Leopold, or "Babe" as his friends knew him, was born in 1906 and, from an early age, had a number of sexual encounters, starting with the advances of a governess and culminating in a relationship with Richard Loeb. He was an excellent student with a genius IQ and was only eighteen when he graduated from the University of Chicago. He was an expert ornithologist and botanist and spoke nine languages fluently. Like that of many burgeoning killers, his family life was totally empty and devoid of control. His mother died when he was young and his father gave him little personal attention. He compensated for his lack of fatherly direction with expensive presents and huge sums of money. Leopold was given $3,000 to tour Europe before entering Harvard Law School, a car of his own and a $125-a-week allowance.

Richard Loeb was the son of the vice-president of Sears & Roebuck, and while he was equally wealthy as his friend, Loeb was merely a clever young man and far from brilliant. He was, however, quite handsome and

Nathan Leopold. *Courtesy of the* Chicago Daily News.

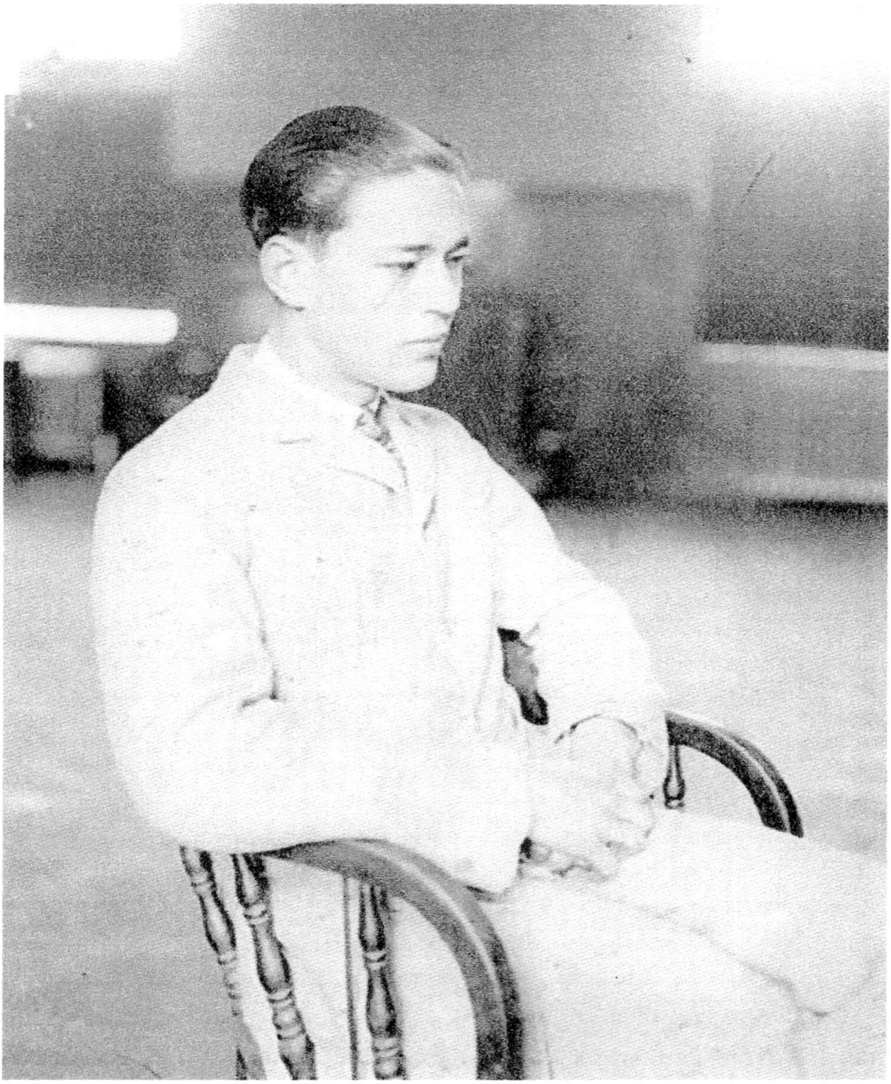

Richard Loeb. *Courtesy of the* Chicago Daily News.

charming, and what he lacked in intelligence, he more than made up for in arrogance. Both of the young men were obsessed with perfection. To them, perfection meant being above all others, a condition that their stations in life endorsed. They felt they were immune to laws and criticism, which meant they were perfect.

Loeb fancied himself a master criminal detective, but his dream was to commit the perfect crime. With his more docile companion in tow, Loeb began developing what he believed to be the perfect scheme. He also constantly searched for ways to control others. Not long after the two became friends, Leopold attempted to initiate a sexual relationship with Loeb. At first, Loeb spurned his friend's advances, but then he offered a compromise. He would engage in sex with Leopold, but only under the condition that the other boy begin a career in crime with him. Leopold agreed, and they signed a formal pact to that effect.

Over the course of the next four years, they committed robbery, vandalism, arson and petty theft, but this was not enough for Loeb. He dreamed of something bigger. The perfect murder, he convinced his friend, would be their greatest intellectual challenge.

They worked out a scheme over the course of the next seven months. The plan was to kidnap someone and then make it appear as though that person was being held for ransom. They would write the ransom note on a typewriter that had been stolen from Loeb's old fraternity house at the University of Michigan and make the family of the victim believe that he would be returned to them. Leopold and Loeb had no such intentions, though. Their only plan was to kill their captive.

In May 1924, they rented a car and drove to a hardware store at Forty-third Street and Cottage Avenue, where they purchased some rope, a chisel and a bottle of hydrochloric acid. They would garrote their victim, stab him with the chisel if necessary and then destroy his identity with the acid.

The next day, they met at Leopold's home and wrapped the handle of the chisel with adhesive tape so that it offered a better grip. They also found a blanket and tore strips of cloth that could be used to wrap up and bind their victim. Leopold also placed a pair of wading boots in the car because the boys planned to deposit the body in the swamps near Wolf Lake, located south of the city. They packed two loaded pistols and looked over the already typed ransom note that demanded $10,000 in cash. Neither of them needed the money, but they felt that the note would convince the authorities that the kidnappers were lowly criminals and deflect attention from people like Leopold and Loeb.

They had only overlooked one thing—a victim.

They first considered killing Loeb's younger brother, Tommy, but they discarded that idea, not because Tommy was a family member, but because it would have been hard for Loeb to collect the ransom money without arousing suspicion. They next considered killing William Deutsch, grandson of millionaire and philanthropist Julius Rosenwald, but dismissed this idea because Rosenwald was the president of Sears & Roebuck and Loeb's father's immediate boss. They also came close to agreeing to kill their friend Richard Rubel, who regularly had lunch with them. He was ruled out too, not because he was a good friend, but because they knew his father was cheap and would never agree to pay the ransom.

They could not agree on anyone but did feel that their victim should be small so that he could be easily subdued. With that in mind, they decided to check out the Harvard Preparatory School, which was located across the street from Leopold's home. They climbed into their rental car and began to drive. As they drove, Leopold noticed some boys near Ellis Avenue, and Loeb pointed out one of them whom he recognized, fourteen-year-old Bobby Franks. He was the son of the millionaire Jacob Franks and a distant cousin of Loeb. Chosen by chance, he would make the perfect victim for the perfect crime.

Bobby was already acquainted with his killers. He had played tennis with Loeb several times and he happily climbed into the car. Although they both later denied being the actual killer, Leopold was at the wheel and Loeb was in the back, gripping the murder weapon tightly in his hands. They drove Bobby to within a few blocks of the Franks residence in Hyde Park and then Loeb suddenly grabbed the boy, stuffed a gag in his mouth and smashed his skull four times with a chisel. The rope had been forgotten. Bobby collapsed onto the floor of the car, unconscious and bleeding badly.

When Leopold saw the blood spurting from Bobby's head, he cried out, "Oh God, I didn't know it would be like this!"

Loeb ignored him, intent on his horrific task. Even though Bobby was unconscious, Loeb stuffed his mouth with rags and wrapped him up in the heavy blanket. The boy continued to bleed for a time and then died.

With the excitement of the actual murder concluded, Leopold and Loeb casually drove south, stopped for lunch and then continued driving for a little while longer. They had supper as they waited for the sun to go down. Eventually, they ended up near a culvert along the Pennsylvania Railroad tracks. It emptied into a swamp along Wolf Lake.

Leopold put on his hip boots and carried Bobby's body to the culvert. They had stripped all of the clothes from his body, and then, after dunking the boy's head underwater to make sure that he was dead, they poured acid on his face in hopes that he would be harder to identify. Leopold then

Murder victim Bobby Franks. *Courtesy of the* Chicago Daily News.

struggled to shove the naked boy into the drainpipe and took his coat off to make the work easier. Unknown to the killers, a pair of eyeglasses were in the pocket of Leopold's coat, and they fell out into the water when he removed it. This would be the undoing of the "perfect crime."

After pushing the body as far into the pipe as he could, Leopold sloshed out of the mud toward the car, where Loeb waited for him. The killers believed that the body would not be found until long after the ransom money had been received. With darkness falling, though, Leopold failed to notice that Bobby's foot was dangling from the end of the culvert.

They drove back to the city and parked the rental car next to a large apartment building. Bobby's blood had soaked through the blanket in which he had been wrapped and had stained the automobile's upholstery. The blanket was hidden in a nearby yard and the boys burned Bobby's clothing at Leopold's house. They typed out the Frankses' address on the already prepared ransom note. After this, they hurried back to the car and drove to Indiana, where they buried the shoes that Bobby had worn and everything that he had on him that was made from metal, including his belt buckle and class pin from the prep school.

Finally, with their "perfect crime" carried out, they drove back to Leopold's home and spent the rest of the evening drinking and playing cards. About midnight, they telephoned the Frankses' home and told Mr. Franks that he could soon expect a ransom demand for the return of his son. "Tell the police and he will be killed at once," they told Mr. Franks. "You will receive a ransom note with instructions tomorrow."

The next morning, the ransom note, signed with the name "George Johnson," was delivered to the Frankses, demanding $10,000 in old, unmarked $10 and $20 bills. The money was to be placed in a cigar box that should be wrapped in white paper and sealed with wax. After the note's arrival, the Frankses' lawyer notified the police, who promised no publicity.

Meanwhile, Leopold and Loeb continued with the elaborate game they had concocted. They took the bloody blanket to an empty lot, burned it and then drove to Jackson Park, where Loeb tore the keys out of his stolen typewriter. He threw the keys into one lagoon in the park and the typewriter into another. Later in the afternoon, Loeb took a train ride to Michigan City, leaving a note addressed to the Frankses in the telegram slot of a stationary desk in the train's observation car. He got off the train at Sixty-third Street when it returned to the city and rejoined Leopold. Andy Russo, a yardman, found the letter and sent it to the Frankses.

Investigators examine the culvert at Wolf Lake where Bobby Franks's body was found. *Courtesy of the* Chicago Daily News.

However, by the time the letter arrived, railroad maintenance men had already stumbled on the body of Bobby Franks. The police notified Jacob Franks and he sent his brother-in-law to identify the body. He confirmed that it was Bobby, and the newspapers went into overdrive, producing "extra" editions that were on the street in a matter of hours.

One of the largest manhunts in the history of Chicago began. Witnesses and suspects were picked up in huge numbers, and slowly the "perfect crime" began to unravel. Despite their "mental prowess" and "high intelligence," Leopold and Loeb were quickly caught. Leopold had dropped his eyeglasses near the spot where the body had been hidden, and police had traced the prescription to Albert Coe & Company, which stated that only three pairs of glasses with such unusual frames had been sold. One pair belonged to an attorney, who was away in Europe, the other to a woman and the third pair to Nathan Leopold.

The boys were brought in for questioning and began supplying alibis for the time when Bobby had gone missing. They had been with two girlfriends, they claimed, "May and Edna." The police asked them to provide contact information for them, but the killers could not. Leopold claimed that he had lost the glasses at Wolf Lake during a recent bird-hunting trip. The detectives noted that it had rained a few days before but the glasses were clean. Could Leopold explain this? He couldn't.

Then, two novice reporters, Al Goldstein and Jim Mulroy, obtained the letters that Richard Loeb had written with the stolen typewriter, which had already been found in Jackson Park. The letters matched the type on the ransom note, which was a perfect match for the typewriter that Leopold had "borrowed" from his fraternity house the year before.

Loeb broke first. He said that the murder was a lark, an experiment in crime to see if the "perfect murder" could be carried out. He then denied being the killer and claimed that he had driven the car while Leopold had slashed Bobby Franks to death. Leopold refuted this. Finally, the boys were brought together and admitted the truth. Loeb had been the killer and Leopold had driven the car, but they had planned the crime together. They were both guilty of Bobby Franks's murder.

The people of Chicago, and the rest of the nation, were stunned. It was fully expected that the two would receive a death sentence for the callous and coldblooded crime.

After the confession, Loeb's family disowned him, but Leopold's father turned to Clarence Darrow, America's most famous defense attorney, in hopes that he might save his son. For a substantial fee, Darrow agreed to seek the best possible verdict that he could, which in this case was life in prison. "While the State is trying Loeb and Leopold," Darrow said, "I will try capital punishment."

Darrow would have less trouble with the case than he would with his clients, who constantly clowned around and hammed it up in the courtroom. Newspaper photographers frequently snapped photos of them smirking and laughing in court, and the public, already turned against them, became even more hostile toward the "poor little rich boys."

Darrow was fighting an uphill battle, but he brought out every trick in the book and used shameless tactics during the trial. He declared the boys to be insane. Leopold, he said, was a dangerous schizophrenic. They weren't criminals, he railed, they just couldn't help themselves. After this weighty proclamation, Darrow actually began to weep. The trial became a landmark in criminal law. He offered a detailed description of what would happen to the boys as they were hanged, providing a graphic image of bodily functions

Leopold, Loeb and attorney Clarence Darrow in the crowded courtroom during the sensational trial. Darrow can be seen just to the left of the judge's head. Leopold and Loeb are standing near the middle of the photograph. *Courtesy of the* Chicago Daily News.

and physical pain. Darrow even turned to the prosecutor and invited him to personally perform the execution.

Darrow's horrifying description had a marked effect on the courtroom and especially on the defendants. Loeb was observed to shudder, and Leopold got so hysterical that he had to be taken out of the courtroom. Darrow wept for the defendants, wept for Bobby Franks and then wept for defendants and victims everywhere. He managed to get the best verdict possible out of the case. The defendants were given life in prison for Bobby Franks's murder and an additional ninety-nine years for his kidnapping.

Ironically, after all of that, Darrow only managed to get less than half of his fee from Leopold's father. He got this after a seven-month wait and the threat of a lawsuit.

Leopold and Loeb were sent to Joliet Prison. Even though the warden claimed that they were treated just like all of the other prisoners, they each enjoyed a private cell, books, a desk, a filing cabinet and even pet birds. They also showered away from the other prisoners and took their meals, which were prepared to order, in the officer's lounge. They were granted any number of unsupervised visitors, and Leopold was allowed to keep a flower garden. The doors to their cells were usually left open, and they had passes to visit each other at any time.

Richard Loeb was eventually killed by another inmate, who claimed that Loeb had been making sexual advances toward him. The inmate, James Day, turned on him in a bathroom and attacked him with a razor. Loeb, covered in blood, managed to make it out of the bathroom and collapsed in the hallway. He was found bleeding in the corridor by guards and died a short time later. It was later discovered that Day had slashed him fifty-six times with the razor.

When Clarence Darrow was told of Loeb's death, he slowly shook his head. "He is better off dead," the great attorney said, "for him, death is an easier sentence."

Leopold lived on in prison for many years and was said to have made many adjustments to his character—some would even say he was rehabilitated completely. Even so, appeals for his parole were turned down three times. Finally, in 1958, the poet Carl Sandburg, who went as far as to offer Leopold a room in his own home, pleaded his fourth appeal. Finally, in March of that year, he was released.

Leopold was allowed to go to Puerto Rico, where he worked among the poor and married a widow named Trudi Feldman Garcia de Quevedo, who owned a flower shop. He went on to write a book about his experiences called *Life Plus 99 Years* and continued to be hounded by the press for his role in the "perfect murder" that he had committed decades before. He stated that he would be "haunted" by what he had done for the rest of his life.

Nathan Leopold died of heart failure on August 30, 1971, bringing to an end one of the most harrowing stories in the history of Chicago.

Death of a Union Leader's Wife

During the early morning hours on the day after St. Patrick's Day 1947, the sound of shotguns echoed in the darkness of the South Shore neighborhood. The deafening roar of the guns was followed by the cries of Chicago Bartender's Union boss James D. Crowley as he realized that his wife had been struck by bullets that had been intended for him. Betty Crowley, soaked in blood, was slumped over the steering wheel of her husband's 1946 Cadillac sedan. She was pronounced dead when the ambulance arrived. Crowley knew that if not for blind luck, it would have been his body that was taken to the Cook County Morgue that night.

James Crowley was the boss of the Local 278 of the Bartender & Beverage Dispensers Union (also known as the Chicago Bartender's Union), and he was greatly admired for his battle against organized crime's influence on the union. Oddly, though, Crowley was often closely involved with gangland figures like Frank Nitti, once known as Al Capone's "enforcer." In fact, when Crowley first ran for the position of local president of the union in 1941, he was dismissed as nothing more than Nitti's candidate. After examining Crowley's past, the state's attorney's office agreed. The labor racketeering squad of the Chicago Police Department called Crowley "a fellow traveler" in mob circles and a man the mob knew would always cooperate. He was allowed to take over the union only under court supervision.

But like many other union tough guys who forged links with organized crime only to kick out the mobsters when they were of no more use to them, Crowley broke with his mob bosses. He denounced all connections with

Frank Nitti was often referred to as Al Capone's "enforcer," but after his boss went to prison for tax evasion, Nitti became one of the public faces of the Chicago Outfit. He often dealt personally with the organization's business with labor unions. *Courtesy of the Chicago Historical Society.*

organized crime and managed to gain power by working with reformers, mostly because it was in his best interests to do so.

Prior to this, though, Crowley and the members of Local 278 had put up with being bled dry by the Chicago Outfit for years. In 1940, the former head of Local 278, George B. McLane, who had his own background as a criminal racketeer, testified that he had been the president of the union for twenty-eight years and was manipulated by Frank Nitti and the outfit from 1935 to 1940 so that the syndicate could take over the union. This testimony led to indictments against Nitti, Paul "the Waiter" Ricca, Murray Humphreys, Thomas Panton, Frederick Evans, Louis Campagna and Louis Romano, an outfit front man and the president of Local 278 after McLane was ousted. The mobsters were indicted by a Cook County grand jury on a conspiracy charge related to their alleged control of the union.

The takeover had its beginnings in 1935 during an outfit meeting at the Capri Restaurant on North Clark Street. During the meeting, Nitti, Campagna, Ricca, Joseph Fusco, Jake Guzik and Fred Evans first leaned on George McLane. Nitti reportedly made a direct death threat to McLane if he didn't cooperate in the takeover of the union.

At the 1940 trial, Nitti and his associates were also accused of installing outfit members in union management positions and forcing the sale of alcohol from mob-controlled breweries. It was claimed that the mob managed to loot more than $1 million in union funds. Nitti personally managed and masterminded the plan, approving all letters and literature used to elect his union candidates. McLane had proved to be stubborn for a time, although at a meeting at the LaSalle Hotel in which McLane refused an offer by Nitti to name a mob union officer, Nitti made a direct threat: "We've taken over the other unions. You'll put our man in, or you will get shot in the head."

The meeting was followed by another gathering at the Capri Restaurant, where Nitti repeated the threat. He told McLane, "Give me the names of any board members who oppose us. We'll take care of them. We want no more playing around. If you don't do like I say, you'll get shot in the head. How would your old lady look in black?"

McLane was no fool. In July 1935, Louis Romano became president of the bartender's local union. Romano was a former Capone gunman and became a Nitti stooge.

Despite the indictments, the outfit bosses walked away from the case against them as free men. McLane was quick to testify before the grand jury, but in open court, he was thoroughly intimidated and refused to testify against Nitti and the others on the convenient grounds that it might incriminate him. Rumor had it that McLane had been promised that if he went through with his testimony, his wife would be mailed to him in small pieces.

McLane may have had a change of heart, but the indictments were incentive enough for James Crowley and the rest of the Local 278 members to shed themselves of the mob. Crowley, who had served under Louis Romano as the secretary-treasurer of the union, was elevated to the top spot. He started building a reputation for himself as he refused to back down to mob threats. Surrounded by his own squad of gunmen, he began to feel more powerful than he actually was.

His newfound sense of power was challenged in the summer of 1946. A group of gangsters, led by Martin "the Ox" Ochs, began traveling to South

Mob president of Local 278 of the Bartender's Union, Louis Romano.

Side taverns, demanding huge advertising funds for a carnival souvenir program that they were peddling. They also demanded from Crowley that tavern owners buy only a certain kind of pretzels and ginger ale, the kind the outfit was distributing all over Chicago. Crowley sent word to his members to refuse to buy the ads or the pretzels, and he dared Ochs to do something about it. Ochs backed down and the gangsters left the bar owners alone. Crowley now seemed invincible.

In 1947, the mob was still working to control the union. Crowley and Dennis Kelly of the Bartender's Union in Joliet were embroiled in a tough election fight to get C.T. McDonough elected secretary-treasurer of the international union, opposing Edward Miller of Kansas City. Crowley was slated for the vice-presidential office of the international, a coveted spot. The election of new officers was scheduled for April. The months leading up to it were bitter and contentious, filled with violence and bloodshed. The police cited the strife over the union elections as the reason behind the St. Patrick's Day assassination attempt against Crowley.

Crowley and his wife, Betty, had married in 1941 and were, by all reports, a devoted couple. They lived in an area known as South Shore, which extended from Sixty-seventh Street south to Seventy-ninth Street and from Stony Island Avenue to the beaches of Lake Michigan. The growth of South Shore was largely the result of upward mobility among the Irish and Germans of Washington Park in the 1920s and 1930s. The closing of the Washington Park racetrack, and its exclusive country club, in 1905 was usually offered as the reason wealthy and upper-middle-class residents left the area, but in truth, the arrival of thousands of black families from the rural South triggered the flight and set up a pattern of racial segregation that continued for decades. South Shore, once a Protestant enclave, absorbed the Irish-Catholic and Jewish populations through the 1920s and 1930s.

The Crowleys lived in an apartment in a brick, two-flat home, located at 7225 South Merrill. On St. Patrick's Day, they attended a swanky party at the Morrison Hotel, where they celebrated a rousing holiday in the company of scores of other Irish revelers. There had been a lot of drinking going on, and Crowley was quite intoxicated by about 8:00 p.m. He was a hard-drinking man, with one intoxicated driving arrest to his name, and he suggested to Betty that it might be a good idea for her to drive them back to the South Side, just to be safe. Mrs. Crowley was completely sober. She had given up alcohol in observance of Lent.

They arrived home at just after 2:15 a.m., and as Betty eased the sedan to a stop at the curb, another automobile sped by and men inside opened fire on the Crowleys' Cadillac with shotguns. Windows shattered, and the force of the blast hit the unlucky woman behind the wheel. Pellets ripped into her face and upper body, and bits of her silver fox coat were scattered all over the interior of the car. Crowley screamed his wife's name, but she did not respond.

Crowley, wounded by the shots, managed to stagger into the apartment and telephone the Grand Crossing District police station before passing out from loss of blood. "Why couldn't it have been me alone?" he asked after regaining consciousness in Wesley Memorial Hospital. "Betty was my best friend."

Betty's murder was never solved, although everyone knew who was responsible. The police recovered cigarette butts at the southwest corner of

Seventy-second Place and Merrill, a sure sign that the killers had been lying in wait for some time, but there was no way to know who had smoked them. However, they were sure to have been left there by outfit gunmen. It wasn't often that gangland killed a woman, even in a moment of carelessness like this one, but for the Chicago Outfit, it was an extreme situation. And since the outfit was unable to get to Crowley in his heavily guarded hospital room, it went after his number two man instead.

On April 2, Dennis Kelly of the Joliet local of the Bartender's Union survived an outfit ambush on Route 66 north of Joliet. A bullet perforated his lung, but he, too, managed to survive.

Although most believed that the murder of Crowley's wife would bring out the sympathy vote among rank and file members, it didn't. Crowley refused to back down. "I'm running for vice president against James P. Blakely and this shot-up arm isn't changing my mind!" he vowed, but surprisingly, the entire Crowley-McDonough slate was soundly defeated. The labor leader faded from history, but he had survived his brush with the mob.

Dennis Kelly was not so lucky. On March 5, 1953, he was mowed down by outfit gunfire in Hammond, Indiana, after leaving the home of his mistress. His killers, just like in the case of Betty Crowley, were never brought to justice.

The Cold Case of the Grimes Sisters

One of the most puzzling unsolved mysteries in Chicago history dates back to a dark winter's night in the mid-1950s, when two young South Side girls vanished for more than three weeks and sent chills down the spines of every parent in the region. Unsettled feelings turned to horror when the bodies of the girls were discovered alongside a rural roadway a short time later. To this date, their killers have not been found.

On December 28, 1956, Patricia Grimes, age thirteen, and Barbara Grimes, age fifteen, left their home at 3624 South Damen Avenue and headed for the Brighton Theatre, only a mile away. The girls were both avid fans of Elvis Presley and on that night were on their way to see his film *Love Me Tender* for the eleventh and what turned out to be final time. The girls were recognized in the popcorn line at 9:30 p.m. and then seen on an eastbound Archer Avenue bus at 11:00 p.m. After that, things became less certain, but this may have been the last time they were ever seen alive. The two sisters were missing for twenty-five days before their naked and frozen bodies were found along German Church Road, just outside the small town of Willow Springs.

The girls' mother, Loretta Grimes, expected them to be home no later than 11:45 p.m. but was already growing uneasy when they had not arrived fifteen minutes prior to that. At midnight, she sent her daughter Theresa and her son, Joey, to the bus stop at Thirty-fifth and Hoyne to watch for them. After three buses had stopped and had failed to discharge their sisters, Theresa and Joey returned home without them. They never saw the girls again, but strangely, others claimed to have seen them.

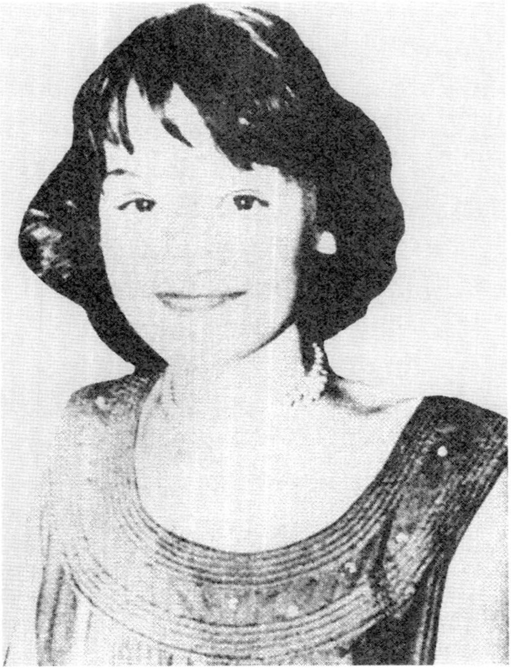

Patricia Grimes. *Courtesy of* Wide World.

Barbara Grimes. *Courtesy of* Wide World.

The last reported sightings of the two girls came from classmates who allegedly spotted them at Angelo's Restaurant at 3551 South Archer Avenue, more than twenty-four hours after their reported disappearance. How accurate this sighting was is unknown because a railroad conductor also claimed to have seen them on a train near the Great Lakes Naval Training Center in north suburban Glenview around the same time. A security guard on the northwest side offered directions to two girls he believed were the Grimes sisters on the morning of the twenty-ninth, hours after they disappeared. On January 1, both girls were allegedly identified as passengers aboard a city bus on Damen Avenue. During the week that followed, they were reported in Englewood by George Pope, a night clerk at the Unity Hotel on West Sixty-first Street, who refused them a room because of their ages. Three employees at Kresge believed they saw the girls listening to Elvis Presley songs at the record counter on January 3.

The police theorized that the girls had run away, but Loretta Grimes refused to believe it. She was sure that the girls had gone missing against their will, but the authorities were not convinced. Regardless, it became the greatest missing persons hunt in Chicago police history. Even Elvis Presley, in a statement issued from Graceland, asked the girls to come home and ease their mother's worries. His plea went unanswered.

More strangeness occurred before the bodies of the girls were found. A series of ransom letters, which were later discovered to have come from a mental patient, took Mrs. Grimes to Milwaukee on January 12. She was escorted by FBI agents and instructed to sit in a downtown Catholic church with $1,000 on the bench beside her. The letter promised that Barbara Grimes would walk in to retrieve the money and then leave to deliver it to the kidnapper. She and her sister would then be released. Needless to say, no one ever came, and Mrs. Grimes was left sitting for hours to contemplate her daughters' fate. By that time, it's likely that the bodies of the two girls were already lying along German Church Road, covered with snow.

But if that's true, then how can we explain the two telephone calls that were received by Wallace and Ann Tollstan on January 14? Their daughter, Sandra, was a classmate of Patricia Grimes at the St. Maurice School, and the Tollstans received the two calls about midnight. The first call jolted Mr. Tollstan out of his sleep, but when he picked up the receiver, the person on the other end of the line did not speak. He waited a few moments and then hung up. About fifteen minutes later, the phone rang again and this time Ann Tollstan answered it. The voice on the other end of the line asked,

"Is that you, Sandra? Is Sandra there?" But before Mrs. Tollstan could bring her daughter to the phone, the caller had clicked off the line. Ann Tollstan was convinced that the frightened voice on the telephone belonged to Patricia Grimes.

The search for the Grimes sisters ended on January 22, 1957, when construction worker Leonard Prescott was driving south on German Church Road early one morning. He spotted what appeared to be two discarded clothing store mannequins lying next to a guardrail, a short distance from the road. A few feet away, the ground dropped off to Devil's Creek below. Unsure of what he had seen, Prescott nervously brought his wife to the spot, and then they drove to the local police station. His wife, Marie Prescott, was so upset by the sight of the bodies that she had to be carried back to their car.

Once investigators realized that the "mannequins" were actually bodies, they soon discovered that they were the Grimes sisters. Barbara lay on her left side with her legs slightly drawn up toward her body. Her head was covered by the body of her sister, who had been thrown onto her back with her head turned sharply to the right. It looked as if they had been discarded there by someone so cold and heartless that he saw the girls as nothing more than garbage to be tossed away on a lonely roadside.

The officials in charge, Cook County sheriff Joseph D. Lohman and Harry Glos, an aggressive investigator for Coroner Walter E. McCarron, surmised that the bodies had been lying there for several days, perhaps as far back as January 9. This had been the date of the last heavy snowfall, and the frigid temperatures that followed the storm had preserved the bodies to a state that resembled how they had looked at the moment of death.

The discovery of the girls' remains sent the various police departments into action. A short time after they were found, more than 160 officers from Chicago, Cook County, the Forest Preserves and five south suburban police departments began combing the woods and, unfortunately, tramping all over whatever evidence may have been there. Between the officers, the reporters, the medical examiners and everyone else, the investigation was already off to a bad start.

Things became even more confusing in the days to come. The bodies were removed from the scene and were taken to the Cook County Morgue, where they would be stored until they thawed out and an autopsy became possible. Before they were removed, though, both police investigators and reporters commented on the condition of the corpses, noting bruises and marks that, to this day, still have not been adequately explained. According to a newspaper article, there were three "ugly" wounds in Patricia's

The location on German Church Road where the bodies of the Grimes sisters were discovered in January 1957.

abdomen, and the left side of her face had been battered, resulting in a possible broken nose. Barbara's face and head had also been bruised and there were punctures from an ice pick in her chest. Once the bodies were moved, investigators stayed on the scene to search for clothing and clues, but nothing was found.

The autopsies were performed on the following day, but any hope that the examinations would provide new evidence or leads was quickly dashed. Despite the efforts of three experienced pathologists, they could not reach agreement on a time or cause of death. They stated that the girls had died from shock and exposure but were only able to reach this conclusion by eliminating other causes. And by also concluding that the girls had died on December 28, the night they had disappeared, they created more mysteries than they managed to solve. If the girls had died on the night they had gone missing, then how could the sightings that took place after that date be explained? And if the bodies had been exposed to the elements since that time, then why hadn't anyone else seen them?

Barbara and Patricia were buried on January 28, one month after they disappeared, although the mystery was no closer to being solved than it had been in December.

The residents of Chicago were stunned, and the case of the murdered girls became an obsession. The local community organized a search for clues, and volunteers passed out flyers looking for information. The *Chicago Tribune* invited readers to send in theories about the case and paid $50 for any it published. The clergy and the parishioners from St. Maurice, where the Grimes family attended church, offered a $1,000 reward and sent out letters to area residents, hoping that someone might have seen the girls before they vanished. In hopes that it might jog the memory of anyone who might have seen them, photographs were taken of friends of the girls wearing the same style and colors of sweaters, jackets and scarves that the Grimes sisters had been wearing on the night they vanished. In spite of all this, no new leads surfaced, and the killer continued to elude the authorities.

Investigators questioned an unbelievable 300,000 people, searching for information about the girls, and 2,000 of these people were seriously interrogated, which in those days could be brutal. A number of suspects were seriously considered, including a seventeen-year-old named Max Fleig. The police believed that he was somehow connected to the case, although the law at that time did not allow juveniles to be tested with a polygraph. Police Captain Ralph Petaque persuaded the boy to take the test anyway, and in the midst of it, he confessed to kidnapping the girls. Because the test was illegal and inadmissible, the police were forced to let Fleig go free. Was he the killer? No one will ever know. Fleig was sent to prison a few years later for the brutal murder of a young woman, but whether he had any connection to the death of the Grimes sisters remains a mystery.

In the midst of all of this, the police still had to deal with nuts and cranks, so-called psychic visions and a number of false confessions, which made their work even harder.

Eager to crack the floundering case, Cook County sheriff Joseph Lohman arrested a skid-row dishwasher named Edward L. "Benny" Bedwell. The drifter, who sported Elvis-style sideburns and a ducktail haircut, had reportedly been seen with the Grimes sisters in a restaurant where he sometimes washed dishes in exchange for food. When he was initially questioned, Bedwell admitted that he had been in the D&L Restaurant on West Madison with two girls and an unnamed friend, but he insisted that the owners of the place were mistaken about the girls being the Grimes sisters.

According to the restaurant owners, John and Minnie Duros, the group had entered the diner about 5:30 a.m. on December 30. They described the taller girl, who Minnie Duros said was wearing a coat with the name "Pat" embroidered on it, as being either so drunk or so sick that she was staggering as she walked. The couples sat in a booth for a while, listened to Elvis songs on the jukebox and then went outside. One of the girls came back in, laid her head on the table and seemed to be sick. The two men eventually managed to get her outside and all of them left together. One of the girls told Minnie Duros that they were sisters.

Lohman found the story plausible, thanks to the unshakable identification of the girls by Minnie Duros, their respective heights, the fact that one of them said they were sisters and, finally, Bedwell's resemblance to Elvis. Lohman believed this might have been enough to get the girls to go along with him. And then of course, there was Bedwell's confession, which related a lurid and sexually explicit tale of drunken debauchery with the two young women. He made and recanted three confessions and even reenacted the crime for investigators on January 27.

Everyone doubted the story but Lohman. He booked Bedwell on murder charges, but the drifter's testimony was both vague and contradictory. On January 31, he testified that he had confessed out of fear of Lohman's men, who had struck and threatened him while he was being questioned. Lohman denied that Bedwell had been beaten. He told newspapers that the drifter had lied when he contradicted his confession and added that he considered Bedwell the prime suspect in the case.

The case against Bedwell further unraveled when his "unnamed friend" was identified as William C. Williamson, who ended up in jail on charges of drunkenness soon after his meeting with Bedwell and the two girls at the Duroses' diner. He admitted that he was with Bedwell and two girls but denied that they were the Grimes sisters.

State's Attorney Benjamin Adamowski ordered the drifter released. Bedwell later spent time in prison on a weapons charge and died at some point after he was released in 1986.

The dismissal of charges against Bedwell in the Grimes case set off another round of bickering among police departments and various jurisdictions, and the case became even more mired in red tape and inactivity. It got even worse when coroner's investigator Harry Glos publicly criticized the autopsy findings concerning the time and cause of death. He shocked the public by announcing that Barbara and Patricia could not have died on the night they disappeared. He said that an ice layer around the bodies proved that they had been warm when they were left along German Church Road and that only after January 7 would there have been enough snow to create the ice and hide the bodies.

Glos also raised the issues of the puncture wounds and bruises on the bodies, which had never been explained or explored. He was sure that the girls had been violently treated prior to death and also asserted that the older sister, Barbara, had been sexually molested before she was killed. The pathologists had denied this, but the Chicago Police crime lab reluctantly confirmed it. However, they were angry with Glos for releasing the information.

The coroner, Walter McCarron, promptly had Glos fired, and many of the other investigators in the case accused him of being reckless and of political grandstanding. Only Sheriff Lohman, who later deputized Glos to work on the case without pay, remained on his side. He agreed that the girls had likely been beaten and tortured by a sexual predator who had lured them into the kidnap car under a seemingly innocent pretense. Lohman remained convinced until his death in 1969 that the predator who had killed the girls was Benny Bedwell.

Other theories maintain that the girls may have indeed encountered Bedwell, or another "older man," and rumors circulated that the reputation of the two girls had been polished to cover up some very questionable behavior on their part. It was said that they sometimes hung around a bar on Archer Avenue where men would buy them drinks. One of the men may have been Benny Bedwell. Harry Glos, who died in 1994, released information that one of the girls had been sexually active, but later reports from those who have seen the autopsy slides say that there is evidence that both of them may have been. It is believed that Coroner McCarron may not have released this information for religious reasons or to spare the family additional grief.

Today, veteran detectives believe there is more to the story than was known in 1957. The general consensus seems to be that Barbara and Patricia may have been abducted by a front man for a "white slavery" ring and taken to a remote location in the woods surrounding Willow Springs. They are convinced that the girls were strangled after refusing to become prostitutes. It's also possible that the girls may have been lured into an involvement in the prostitution ring by someone they knew, not realizing what would be required of them, and that they were killed to keep them silent.

Others refused to even consider this, though, and were angered by the negative gossip about the two girls. Some remain angry about this even today, maintaining that Barbara and Patricia were nice, ordinary, happy girls and were tragically killed on a cold night because they made the mistake of accepting a ride from a stranger. They didn't hang around in bars, these old friends maintain; they were simply innocent teenage girls, just like everyone else at that time.

Perhaps those old acquaintances were right. There are few stories as tragic as the demise of the Grimes sisters, and perhaps it provides some cold comfort for us to believe that their deaths were simply a terrible mistake or the actions of a deviant killer. It can provide us the comfort of knowing that the girls were simply in the wrong place at the wrong time and that such a thing could have happened to anyone. But does believing this make us feel better—or worse?

Now, more than fifty years later, the mystery of who killed the Grimes sisters remains unsolved. As there is no statute of limitations for murder, the case officially remains open, but hope of any closure has dimmed over the years, and the murderer's trail has gone tragically cold.

RICHARD SPECK—BORN TO RAISE HELL

On the hot summer night of July 13, 1966, a brutal and dimwitted drifter butchered his way into the annals of Chicago crime with the murders of eight nursing students on the South Side of the city. From that point on, the name Richard Speck would strike terror in the hearts of young women living alone, and few would ever forget the words inked onto his arm as a burning tattoo.

"Born to Raise Hell," the tattoo read, and it was a fitting description of his life.

Richard Speck was born in Kirkwood, Illinois, in December 1941, the seventh of eight children. Over the years, dozens have speculated about the reason behind Speck's brutal crimes and whether he turned evil somewhere along the way or if he was simply born bad, as the tattoo on his arm suggested. Many have also wondered if perhaps things might have turned out differently in the lives of the eight nursing students if Speck's father, whom he adored, had not died when Speck was only six years old. Speck was raised by his mother in a strict Baptist setting that forbade alcohol and worldly influences. She later married Carl Lindberg, a violent man with an arrest record, and they moved to Dallas, Texas, where Lindberg began taking out his rages on his stepson. By this time, Speck was a slow-witted failure with schoolwork and on the fast track to nowhere. He started running with some older boys, drinking, fighting and getting into trouble.

In November 1962, Speck married Shirley Malone, and they had a daughter, Bobby Lynn, soon after. Their marital bliss was short-lived, however, and Speck began abusing both his wife and his mother-in-law.

Brutal killer Richard Speck in 1966.

According to Shirley's later accounts, he often raped her at knifepoint, claiming that he needed sex four to five times each day. Likely to Shirley's relief, Speck ended up in jail for theft and check fraud in 1963. He was paroled in January 1965 but, after only four weeks, was arrested again for aggravated assault. He was sentenced to serve another sixteen months but was released after only six. Shirley filed for divorce in January 1966.

When Speck was arrested again for burglary and assault, he fled from Dallas with the help of his sister, Carolyn, and left for Chicago. Speck showed up on the doorstep of another sister, Martha, and his brother-in-law, Gene Thornton. Speck announced his intentions to search for work as a merchant seaman, but after several days of doing nothing, Thornton got frustrated and drove his unwanted houseguest to the National Maritime Union Hall, located at 2315 East 100th Street. The building was located just a few doors away from three residential town houses that had been rented by the South Chicago Community Hospital for 24 of its 155 student nurses.

Thornton brought Speck to the Maritime Union Hall because he had heard there was still an open berth on a ship that was bound for Vietnam. The position went to a man with greater seniority, though, leaving Speck without a spot. Disappointed, but unwilling to take Speck back in, Thornton handed him twenty-five dollars and wished him well. He then drove off and left his brother-in-law to fend for himself.

A short time later, Speck managed to get a position aboard an iron ore ship on the Great Lakes, but he was stricken with appendicitis and hospitalized in Hancock, Michigan. When he returned to Chicago in mid-June, he was fired for being drunk and disorderly. He had been warned repeatedly about his drinking and violent behavior, but he disregarded the threats. After that, he spent the next three weeks in cheap hotels, sleeping in the park and financing his liquor and his visits to prostitutes with whatever odd jobs he could find.

On July 13, a depressed and angry Speck was drinking heavily in the Shipyard Inn on the South Side. After consuming a volatile combination of pills and liquor, he suddenly got the urge to "raise some hell." He would later claim that he remembered nothing that he did after this point.

Speck left the bar with a hunting knife, a pocketknife and a borrowed .22-caliber pistol and walked over to one of the nearby student dormitories, number 2319. For the past several weeks, the drifter had seen the women coming and going from the buildings, sunbathing in Luella Park and walking back and forth to their classes. He was familiar enough with their schedules to know that at nearly 11:00 p.m. they would be home in bed.

Corazon Amurao, who shared a second-floor bedroom with two other young women, answered a loud knock on the town house door. She found a tall, lean stranger standing on the doorstep. He smelled of liquor and had a knife in one hand and a gun in the other. He slurred that he was not going to hurt her. "I'm only going to tie you up," he said. "I need money to go to New Orleans."

He shoved his way into the town house and ordered three Filipino students, Valentina Paison, Merlita Garguilo and Corazon, into a bedroom at the back of the building, where Pamela Wilkening, Nina Schmale and Pat Matusek were getting ready for bed. Speck took the sheets from the beds and

The town house at 2319 East 100th Street where eight student nurses were murdered by Richard Speck.

cut them into strips, which he used to bind the women by their wrists and ankles. At 11:30, a seventh nurse, Gloria Davy, returned home from a date, and she was also tied up. Then, a half hour later, Suzanne Farris and her friend Mary Ann Jordan came to the front door. Speck pulled them inside and led them into the back bedroom at gunpoint.

In the course of an hour, Speck had systematically tied and gagged each of the women. How he managed to do this with almost no resistance remains one of the great unsolved mysteries of Chicago crime. Why did none of the women try to escape? Why didn't they try to overpower Speck as he was tying another victim? Why did none of the women in the other town houses hear anything that was taking place? No one knows, and to this day the questions remain unanswered.

By 3:30 a.m., Speck's lust was finally spent. One by one, he had taken the eight young women out of the bedroom and killed them. Only one of them, Gloria Davy, had been raped, but all were dead—except for Cora Amurao, who had managed to roll under a bunk bed and cower there in fear and shock until Speck finally left. Amurao remained hidden, frozen in terror, until daybreak. When she finally emerged from her hiding place, she climbed out of the apartment window and, perched on a ledge, began to scream.

Her screams caught the attention of Judy Dykton, a student who lived across the street. She had gotten up early to study and was startled by the cries from outside. Snatching her robe, she ran over to find Cora shaking and crying on the window ledge. Judy entered the open door of the town house and stepped into the living room. She first discovered the naked body of Gloria Davy, her hands tied behind her and a strip of cloth wrapped tightly around her throat. Her cold skin had turned a dusty blue color. She was obviously dead. Dykton turned and fled to the apartment of the housemother, Mrs. Bisone.

The housemother woke up the other student nurses and ran from the house toward 2319. With her, she brought Leona Bonczak, who entered the house. Bonczak first checked to see if Gloria showed any signs of life and then mounted the stairs and looked down the hall. In the bathroom, she found the body of Pat Matusek and then crept into the other bedrooms, where she discovered the rest of the students so drenched in blood that she was unable to recognize any of them, except for Nina Schmale. A pillow covered most of the girl's face, but she lay on her back, hands tied behind her, a cloth around her neck, legs spread apart and a fatal knife wound to her heart.

Stunned, Bonczak went downstairs and numbly told Mrs. Bisone that everyone was dead. The housemother, shaking and sick, picked up the phone, called South Chicago Community Hospital and told them that all of her girls had been murdered. When the hospital asked her who had been killed, she was unable to tell them. The only words she uttered were "Send help!"

Someone on the street managed to flag down police officer Daniel Kelly, a young patrolman who had only been on the job for eighteen months. He radioed in that there was trouble and then entered the house. He was shocked to discover the body of Gloria Davy in the living room. Kelly had once dated Gloria's sister. Upset, he drew his gun, searched the place and found the other bodies. The town house looked like a charnel house, and in places, the blood in the carpeting was so thick that it pooled over Kelly's shoes. He ran outside to his car radio and called it in. Soon, Kelly heard the comforting sounds of approaching sirens beginning to fill the air.

The street outside filled with police cars and cops, and people ran from door to door, alerting their neighbors of the horror found in 2319. The first detective on the scene was Jack Wallenda, who was shocked by the utter brutality of the killings. He entered the house and viewed the bodies one by one.

He found Gloria first. She was nude, belly down on the couch and tied with double-knotted bedsheets. He noticed what appeared to be semen between her buttocks and found buttons from her blouse strewn down the stairs. The killer had apparently torn them off of her as he pulled her to the living room. Also tossed on the floor was a man's white T-shirt.

Wallenda then checked the upstairs bedroom and found the body of Pamela Wilkening. She had been gagged and stabbed through the heart. Suzanne Farris lay nearby in a pool of blood, and a white nurse's stocking had been twisted around her neck. The detective counted eighteen stab wounds to her chest and neck. He studied Mary Ann Jordan next. She had been stabbed three times in the chest and once in the neck.

In the northwest bedroom, he found Nina Schmale with her nightgown pulled up to her breasts and her legs pulled apart. She had also been tied and stabbed, and it looked as though her neck might be broken. Valentina Paison was found under a blue cover, lying face down. Her throat had been cut. Tossed carelessly on top of her was the body of Merlita Garguilo, who had been stabbed and strangled.

Wallenda walked out the door and to the right and saw the legs of Patricia (Pat) Matusek protruding from the bathroom. She was lying on her back with her hands bound behind her. She had been strangled with a piece of the bedsheet, double knotted, and her nightgown had been dragged up over her breasts. Her white panties had been pulled down to expose her pubic hair. Blood-soaked towels were strewn all over the bathroom floor.

Wallenda's hands were shaking as he left the town house. It was the worst crime scene that he had ever witnessed.

The police immediately went to work and, within hours, were on the trail of Richard Speck. Cora, although heavily sedated, had managed to give an excellent description of the killer, and a nearby gas station attendant remembered one of his managers talking about a guy of the same description who had recently complained about missing a ship and losing out on a job. Police sketch artist Otis Rathel put together an uncanny likeness of Speck. Investigators took the sketch to the Maritime Union Hall and questioned the agent in charge. He remembered an irate seaman who had lost out on a double booking (two guys sent for one job), and he fished the crumpled assignment sheet from the wastebasket. The sheet gave the name of Richard Speck.

After the murders, Speck moved from bar to bar, drinking himself into oblivion, not knowing that the police were on his trail. Detectives had convinced the agent at the Maritime Hall to call Speck's last known telephone number, his sister's, to tell him that he was needed to ship out. The agent connected with Gene Thornton, who agreed to try and track Speck down. He managed to find Speck at the Shipyard Inn and told him that the union hall had a job for him. Speck called the union hall and was told to come down for an assignment on a ship that Speck knew had shipped out several days before. Suspecting a trick, he told the agent that he was up north and it would take him at least an hour to get there. He never showed up.

Immediately, Speck went upstairs, packed his bags and called a cab. He waited in the tavern, playing pool. Three detectives came in looking for a tall blond man with a southern accent. The bartender was no help, and Speck stayed quiet, listening and shooting pool just ten feet away from them. When the cab arrived, Speck refused to give the driver an address and told him he wanted to go to his sister's house, which he said was in a poor and slummy section of town. The cabbie drove north and again asked Speck for an address. Clueless, he pointed to a building that turned out to be part of the Cabrini Green housing project. He got out of the cab and watched the cabbie drive away.

Speck started walking and ended up on Dearborn Street at the Raleigh Hotel, a flophouse that had once been a luxury apartment building. A desk clerk later recalled a drunken Speck coming in with a prostitute. Just before the elevator door closed, he heard the girl call him Richard. A half hour later, the girl came back downstairs and told the clerk that her "date" had a gun. This prompted a call to the police, and two officers from the Eighteenth District police station showed up at the hotel at 8:30 a.m. Speck, still drunk, awoke to find two cops standing over him. He had the gun tucked into the waistband of his pants, and when asked why he had it, he told the officers that it belonged to the prostitute. When asked what his name was, he told them that it was Richard Speck. They checked his wallet and found his seaman's ID and passport, but unfortunately, not all of the police had been notified of the identity of the student nurses' killer yet. Speck was questioned for fifteen minutes, and the officers confiscated the gun but never reported the incident. When they left the hotel, they told the desk clerk that he was "harmless."

Not realizing that Speck had narrowly escaped capture, the police searched the South Side. They managed to track him from the Shipyard Inn to the cab company and then to Cabrini Green. But while they canvassed the housing project, Speck drank himself into another stupor. Later in the afternoon, he ran into some old friends, who suggested that he hop a freight train with them and head out of town. Speck went back to the Raleigh, packed his bags and, on his way out, told the manager that he was going to do some laundry. He never returned. Just fifteen minutes after he walked out, two detectives came in and flashed a photo of Speck in front of the manager. His eyes widened, and he told the officers that Speck had just left.

Oblivious, Speck headed for the Starr Hotel, a run-down dive on West Madison Street that offered temporary refuge to winos and bums. The "rooms" were nothing more than cubicles that were divided by plywood and had "doors" made from chicken wire. For the rate of ninety cents per night, the occupant was provided with a cot, a wall locker, a metal stool and a fifteen-watt bulb that dangled from the ceiling on a wire. In the cramped spaces, drunks could sleep off a hangover amidst the sounds of coughing and moaning and the smells of sweat, booze and vomit. It was the last rung on the ladder for the dregs of humanity.

Speck tossed his bags on a cot and went out to sell some of his belongings to raise money for another night of drinking. He picked up some wine at a local liquor store and spotted several newspapers with his name and photo splashed across them. Speck stumbled back to the Starr Hotel and finished off the entire bottle of wine. He then walked down the hall to the bathroom, smashed the wine bottle and then used the broken glass to cut his wrist and inner elbow. Blood dripped onto the floor as Speck wobbled down the corridor to his cubicle. He collapsed onto the bed, still bleeding badly, and then called out to his neighbors for water and help. They ignored him.

An anonymous call was made to the police but no patrol car was sent. Eventually, Speck was taken to Cook County Hospital. The ambulance drivers ignored Speck's cries for water and missed the police bulletin on their dashboard that had the injured man's photo on it. In the emergency room, nurse Kathy O'Connor prepped Speck and first-year resident Leroy Smith checked his wounds. Smith noticed something familiar about the man. He checked Speck's arm, looking for a tattoo, and found, as he suspected, the inked "Born to Raise Hell." He compared a newspaper photo with the man and realized that he had the killer on his table.

Speck pleaded with the young man for water but Smith grabbed him by the back of the neck and squeezed it as hard as he could. "Did you give water to those nurses?" he demanded. He dropped Speck's head back onto the gurney and called in a policeman who was guarding another patient down the hall. He told him that Richard Speck, the suspect in the murders, was there on the table. The stunned officer started making telephone calls, and all hell broke loose.

Speck was in police custody a few hours later, and William J. Martin, a young and hardworking state's attorney, was faced with putting together and trying the case. He based most of it on the sincere and compelling testimony of Corazon Amurao, who had to be persuaded to remain in the United States long enough to secure the conviction of the monster who had killed her friends. She was understandably unhinged from her ordeal, and she wanted nothing more than to return to the Philippines to try to forget the horrific experience. Martin brought her mother and a cousin to Chicago for moral support and kept them in a secret location away from the press. Her quiet testimony galvanized the courtroom and convinced the jury to convict Speck in just forty-nine minutes. He was given the death sentence for the murders.

Although sentenced to die in the electric chair, the Illinois Supreme Court voided the death penalty in 1971, and Speck was back in court again. This time, he was sentenced to four hundred to twelve hundred years at the Stateville Penitentiary in Joliet. It was the longest prison sentence ever given to an Illinois inmate.

During his incarceration, Speck never admitted his guilt in the murders. He died on December 5, 1991, from a massive heart attack. His autopsy showed that he had an enlarged heart and occluded arteries—he had blown up to 220 pounds by the time of his death. No one claimed his body and he was cremated. His ashes were disposed of in an undisclosed location.

But unfortunately, in 1996, Speck returned.

In May of that year, television journalist Bill Kurtis went behind the walls of Stateville Prison and came back with a secret videotape (originally filmed in the mid-1980s) that showed a bizarre Richard Speck with women's breasts—apparently from hormone treatments—wearing blue panties and having sex with another inmate. Segments of the video, which also showed sex and drug orgies, were shown on the program *American Justice*, and it plunged the Illinois Department of Corrections into a major scandal. Viewers were as repulsed to see what had become of Speck as they were by his bloody crimes.

Even after death, he was still raising hell.

Bibliography

Adler, Jeffrey S. *First in Violence, Deepest in Dirt*. Cambridge, MA: Harvard University Press, 2006.

Asbury, Herbert. *Gem of the Prairie*. New York: Alfred A. Knopf, 1940.

Bilek, Arthur J. *The First Vice Lord*. Nashville, TN: Cumberland House, 2008.

Binder, John J. *The Chicago Outfit*. Chicago: Arcadia, 2003.

Chicago Historical Society

Chicago Public Library

Cowdery, Ray. *Capone's Chicago*. Lakeville, MN: Northstar Commemoratives, 1987.

Demaris, Ovid. *Captive City*. New York: Lyle Stuart, 1969.

Eghigian, Mars, Jr. *After Capone*. Nashville, TN: Cumberland House, 2006.

Farr, Finis. *Chicago*. New Rochelle, NY: Arlington House, 1973.

Franke, David. *The Torture Doctor*. New York: Avon, 1975.

Griffith, William. *Fatal Drop*. Decatur, IL: Whitechapel Press, 2008.

Halper, Albert. *The Chicago Crime Book*. Cleveland, OH: World Publishing, 1967.

Helmer, William. *Public Enemies*. New York: Facts on File, 1998.

Helmer, William, and Arthur J. Bilek. *The St. Valentine's Day Massacre*. Nashville, TN: Cumberland House, 2004.

Humble, Ronald D. *Frank Nitti*. Fort Lee, NJ: Barricade Books, 2007.

Johnson, Curt, with R. Craig Sautter. *Wicked City*. Highland Park, IL: December Press, 1994.

Keefe, Rose. *Guns and Roses*. Nashville, TN: Cumberland House, 2003.

———. *The Man Who Got Away*. Nashville, TN: Cumberland House, 2005.

Kobler, John. *Capone*. New York: G.P. Putnam's Sons, 1971.

Lait, Jack, and Lee Mortimer. *Chicago Confidential*. New York: Crown Publishers, 1950.

Landesco, John. *Organized Crime in Chicago*. Chicago: University of Chicago Press, 1968.

Larson, Erik. *The Devil in the White City*. New York: Crown, 2003.

Lesy, Michael. *Murder City*. New York: W.W. Norton & Co., 2007.

Lewis, Lloyd, and Henry Justin Smith. *Chicago*. New York: Harcourt, Brace & Co., 1929.

Lindberg, Richard. *Chicago by Gaslight*. Chicago: Chicago Academy Publishers, 1996.

———. *Return Again to the Scene of the Crime*. Nashville, TN: Cumberland House, 2001.

———. *Return to the Scene of the Crime*. Nashville, TN: Cumberland House, 1999.

McPhaul, Jack. *Johnny Torrio: First of the Ganglords*. New Rochelle, NY: Arlington House, 1970.

Nash, Jay Robert. *Bloodletters and Bad Men*. New York: M. Evans and Company, Inc., 1995.

———. *Open Files*. New York: McGraw-Hill Book Co., 1983.

Schechter, Harold. *Depraved*. New York: Pocket, 1994.

Sifakis, Carl. *Encyclopedia of American Crime*. New York: Facts on File, 1982.

Taylor, Troy. *Bloody Chicago*. Decatur, IL: Whitechapel Press, 2006.

———. *Bloody Illinois*. Decatur, IL: Whitechapel Press, 2008.

———. *Dead Men Do Tell Tales*. Decatur, IL: Whitechapel Press, 2008.

Wright, Sewell Peaslee. *Chicago Murders*. New York: Duell, Sloan & Pierce, 1945.

NEWSPAPERS

Chicago American
Chicago Daily News
Chicago Herald-American
Chicago Herald & Examiner
Chicago Inter-Ocean
Chicago Sun-Times
Chicago Times
Chicago Tribune

About the Author

Troy Taylor is the author of more than sixty books on history, crime, mystery and the supernatural in America. He was born and raised in Illinois and currently resides in Decatur, Illinois, which was called "one of the most corrupt cities in the state" during the 1920s.